SHEPHERD'S NOTES

SHEPHERD'S NOTES

When you need a guide through the Scriptures

Isaiah

Nashville, Tennessee

Shepherd's Notes— *Isaiah*

Nashville, Tennessee

Printed in the United States of America

Dewey Decimal Classification: 224.107
Subject Heading: BIBLE O.T. ISAIAH
Library of Congress Card Catalog Number: 98–27121

Library of Congress Cataloging-in-Publication Data

Enns, Paul P., 1937–
Isaiah / Paul Enns, editor [i.e. author].
p. cm. — (Shepherd's notes)
Includes bibliographical references.
ISBN 0–8054–9197–X (trade paper)
1. Bible. O.T. Isaiah—Study and teaching. I. Title. II. Series.
BS1515.5.E56 1998
224'.107—dc21

98–27121
CIP

1 2 3 4 5 6 03 02 01 00 99 98

Contents

FOREWORD

Dear Reader:

Shepherd's Notes are designed to give you a quick, step-by-step overview of every book of the Bible. They are not meant to be substitutes for the biblical text; rather, they are study guides intended to help you explore the wisdom of Scripture in personal or group study and to apply that wisdom successfully in your own life.

Shepherd's Notes guide you through the main themes of each book of the Bible and illuminate fascinating details through appropriate commentary and reference notes. Historical and cultural background information brings the Bible into sharper focus.

Six different icons, used throughout the series, call your attention to historical-cultural information, Old Testament and New Testament references, word pictures, unit summaries, and personal application for everyday life.

Whether you are a novice or a veteran at Bible study, I believe you will find *Shepherd's Notes* a resource that will take you to a new level in your mining and applying the riches of Scripture.

In Him,

David R. Shepherd
Editor-in-Chief

How to Use This Book

DESIGNED FOR THE BUSY USER

Shepherd's Notes for Isaiah is designed to provide an easy-to-use tool for getting a quick handle on this Bible book's important features, and for gaining an understanding of the message of Isaiah. Information available in more difficult-to-use reference works has been incorporated into the *Shepherd's Notes* format. This brings you the benefits of many more advanced and expensive works packed into one small volume.

Shepherd's Notes are for laymen, pastors, teachers, small group leaders and participants, as well as the classroom student. Enrich your personal study or quiet time. Shorten your class or small group preparation time as you gain valuable insights into the truths of God's Word that you can pass along to your students or group members.

DESIGNED FOR QUICK ACCESS

Those with time constraints will especially appreciate the time-saving features built into the *Shepherd's Notes*. All features are intended to aid a quick and concise encounter with the heart of the message.

Concise Commentary. Isaiah is unique among the Old Testament writings and deserves to be read and studied over a lifetime. *Shepherd's Notes* provides you with an overview of Isaiah and will enable you to find sections and passages where you would like to spend more time. Short sections provide quick "snapshots" of passages, highlighting important points and other information.

Outlined Text. A comprehensive outline covers the entire text of Isaiah. This is a valuable feature for following the narrative's flow, allowing for a quick, easy way to locate a particular passage.

Shepherd's Notes. These summary statements appear at the close of every key section of the narrative. While functioning in part as a quick summary, they also deliver the essence of the message presented in the sections they cover.

Icons. Various icons in the margin highlight recurring themes in Isaiah, aiding in selective searching or tracing of those themes.

Sidebars and Charts. These specially selected features provide additional background information to your study or preparation. These include definitions as well as cultural, historical, and biblical insights.

Maps. These are placed at appropriate places in the book to aid your understanding and study of a text or passage.

Questions to Guide Your Study. These thought-provoking questions and discussion starters are designed to encourage interaction with the truth and principles of God's Word.

In addition to the above features, study aids have been included at the back of the book for those readers who desire more information and resources for working through Isaiah. These include chapter outlines for studying Isaiah and a list of reference sources used for this volume which offer many works that allow the reader to extend the scope of his or her study of this book.

DESIGNED TO WORK FOR YOU

Personal Study. Using the *Shepherd's Notes* with a passage of Scripture can enlighten your study and take it to a new level. At your fingertips is information that would require searching several volumes to find. In addition, many points of application occur throughout the volume, contributing to personal growth.

Teaching. Outlines frame the text of Isaiah, providing a logical presentation of the message. Shepherd's Notes provide summary statements for presenting the essence of key points and events. Personal Application icons point out personal application of the message of Isaiah, and Historical Context icons indicate where background information is supplied.

Group Study. *Shepherd's Notes* can be an excellent companion volume to use for gaining a quick but accurate understanding of the message of a Bible book. Each group member can benefit by having his or her own copy. The *Note's* format accommodates the study of or the tracing of the themes throughout Isaiah. Leaders may use its flexible features to prepare for group sessions, or use during group sessions. Questions to Guide Your Study can spark discussion of the key points and truths of Isaiah.

LIST OF MARGIN ICONS USED IN ISAIAH

Shepherd's Notes. Placed at the end of each section, a capsule statement provides the reader with the essence of the message of that section.

Historical Context. To indicate background information—historical, biographical, cultural—and provide insight on the understanding or interpretation of a passage.

Old Testament Reference. To indicate other Old Testament passages that illuminate a passage in Isaiah.

New Testament Reference. To indicate a New Testament prophecy fulfillment and its discussion in the text.

Personal Application. Used when the text provides a personal or universal application of truth.

Word Picture. Indicates that the meaning of a specific word or phrase is illustrated so as to shed light on it.

INTRODUCTION

Isaiah, Yesha' Yahu, means "Yahweh [Jehovah] is salvation."

TITLE

The title of the book is taken from the name of the prophet, *Yesha' Yahu*, meaning "Yahweh [Jehovah] is salvation." The theme of the book relates to the name of Isaiah, since Isaiah's message reveals that salvation is by the grace of God.

AUTHORSHIP

Cyrus the Great

Cyrus assumed the throne of Persia about 550 B.C. He was raised by a shepherd after his grandfather tried to kill him after dreaming that Cyrus would one day succeed him as king. As an adult, Cyrus organized the Persians into an army and revolted against his grandfather and his father. He defeated them and claimed the throne.

Traditionally the authorship of the book has been unanimously attributed to Isaiah the prophet. In the late eighteenth century, liberal critics began to deny the unity of Isaiah; they argued that chapters 40–66 were written 150 years later by an unnamed prophet who lived in Babylon during the Exile. This was known as "Second Isaiah." In a later development, liberals argued that chapters 56–66 were written by still another individual, establishing the theory of "Trito-Isaiah."

The basis for the denial of the unity of Isaiah was a philosophical presupposition—antisupernaturalism. The liberal critics rejected the belief that it was possible to predict future events. Hence, since pasages like Isaiah 44:28 and 45:1 predicted Cyrus would rebuild Jerusalem, they assumed these passages were written after the fact.

Of course, Christianity is, at its heart, supernatural. A key claim of Christian faith is the bodily resurrection of Jesus Christ. God, who created and sustains this universe, who raised Jesus Christ from death, is certainly capable of revealing future events in detail to His prophets. Jesus Himself predicted future events (cp. Matt. 24–25). So the prophecies of Isaiah, written by the prophet, can readily be accepted.

The unity of Isaiah has been well established (cp. Gleason Archer, Jr., *A Survey of Old Testament Introduction*; O. T. Allis, *The Unity of Isaiah*; E. J. Young, *Who Wrote Isaiah?*). The following is evidence of the unity of Isaiah:

1. The language is similar throughout both chapters 1–39 and 40–66. The term "the Holy One of Israel" is found twelve times in chapters 1–39 and fourteen times in chapters 40–66. Forty or fifty sentences or phrases appear in both parts of the book (Archer, *A Survey of O.T. Introduction*, pp. 332–334).
2. Both parts of Isaiah reflect the same sins and evil. Both sections mention falsehood (10:1; 59:4–9), bloodshed and violence (1:15; 59:3, 7), hypocrisy (29:13; 58:2, 4), and idolatry (1:29; 57:5).
3. The New Testament quotes Isaiah in a way that suggests both sections were written by Isaiah. John 12:38–40 quotes from 53:1 and 6:9 under the words, "The word of Isaiah the prophet." In Romans 9:27–33 Paul quotes from Isaiah 10:22–23 and 1:9. In Romans 10:16–21 Paul quotes Isaiah 53:1 and 65:1 under the introduction "Isaiah says."
4. The writer had a knowledge of Palestine, mentioning Palestinian trees (44:14; 41:19); yet he showed a lack of knowledge of the land and religion of Babylon.
5. The walls of Jerusalem are still standing (62:6) and the Judean cities are in existence (40:9; 43:6; 48:1–5), indicating this was prior to Nebuchadnezzar's invasions which began in 605 B.C.

Isaiah the prophet, the son of Amoz (1:1), was married to a prophetess (8:1), with a son, Mahershalalhashbaz (8:3). He also had a son, Shearjashub (7:3), possibly by a previous wife. His tribe is unknown. He lived in Jerusalem and had a lengthy ministry to the Southern Kingdom of Judah (ca. 740–680 B.C.). Since King Hezekiah sent his highest officers and elders to meet with Isaiah, it appears the prophet held a high rank in Jerusalem (cp. 2 Kings 19:2).

DATE

The opening statement of Isaiah indicates the date Isaiah was written. Isaiah was written during the reigns of Uzziah (791–740 B.C.), Jotham (750–736 B.C.), Ahaz (736–716 B.C.), and Hezekiah (716–687 B.C.). Isaiah had a lengthy ministry, generally considered from 740–680 B.C.

HISTORICAL SETTING

Several foreign nations impinged on Israel during the time of Isaiah's ministry (740–680 B.C.) and in the centuries following.

Assyria was the major world power during Isaiah's ministry. In 743 B.C. Tiglath-pileser moved south, capturing cities like Carchemish, Hamath, Tyre, Byblos, and others (2 Kings 15:19–20). In 734 B.C. he conquered the Phoenician coast, receiving tribute from Ashkelon and Gaza. King Pekah of Israel (752–732 B.C.) opposed Assyria by forming an alliance with Rezin, king of Syria (Isa. 7). This led to Tiglath-pileser's third invasion in 732 B.C. in which he conquered Damascus and killed Rezin. Hoshea assassinated Pekah and was installed as a puppet of Assyria (2 Kings 17:1–6). In 724 B.C. Shalmaneser V of Assyria invaded Israel (2 Kings 17:3–6), besieging the capital of Samaria from 724–722 B.C. This marked the end of the Northern Kingdom of Israel as the ten northern tribes were taken captive into Assyria in 722/721 B.C.

When Sennacherib ascended the Assyrian throne in 701 B.C., King Hezekiah of Judah joined with Tyre, Egypt, and others in opposing Assyria. As a result, Sennacherib invaded in 701 B.C., crushing the coastal opposition. Hezekiah saw the dilemma and quickly paid tribute to Assyria. However, the Assyrians intimidated the people of Judah, conquering 46 Judean cities and taking 200,000 Judeans captive. But as Hezekiah sought help from the Lord and Isaiah intervened, the Lord slew 185,000 Assyrians overnight and Sennacherib returned to Assyria (see chaps. 36–39).

Babylon was a minor power in Isaiah's day but figured in Judah's future. Under Nabopolassar, the Babylonians defeated the Assyrians in 612 B.C. Nabopolassar's son, Nebuchadnezzar (605–562 B.C.), invaded Judah three times, in 605, 597, and 586 B.C., when Jerusalem was

Babylon was ultimately destroyed in 539 B.C. by the Medo-Persians under Cyrus, who issued a decree, enabling the Jews to return to their homeland. Isaiah had prophesied of Cyrus's decree 150 years earlier (44:28; 45:1).

ultimately destroyed and the two southern tribes in Judah were taken captive to Babylon.

PURPOSE AND THEME

The book of Isaiah follows the twofold theme common to the prophets—judgment and blessing. Chapters 1–39 detail the sins of Judah and Jerusalem and warn the nation of the Lord's judgment. Chapters 40–66 detail the second message—the blessing of restoration in the future. This section is rich in messianic prophecies of the One who will ultimately deliver Israel and inaugurate the millennial reign of righteousness for repentant Israel (42:1–9; 49:1–13; 50:4–11; 52:13–53:12).

Although Isaiah was ministering to the Southern Kingdom of Judah, the term *Israel* occurs with frequency in the biblical text, indicating it is used interchangeably with the people of Judah.

PROPHECIES AGAINST JUDAH (1:1–12:6)

A major function of the prophet was to call the people and the nation back to the covenant relationship under the Mosaic Law through which they were bound to the Lord (Exod. 19). In this first cycle of chapters 1–12, Isaiah condemned Judah for the sin of forsaking the law and pronounced judgment on the apostate nation. But mingled with the judgments are promises of future blessing under the Messiah (cp. 2:1–4).

The nation was bound to the Lord through the Mosaic Covenant whereby the people were obligated to fulfill the demands of the Mosaic Law. The Law specified that obedience brings blessing (Deut. 28:1–14) and disobedience brings chastisement (Deut. 28:15–68).

CONDEMNATION AGAINST JUDAH (1:1–31)

Introduction (1:1)

The introduction defines the scope of Isaiah's ministry: he prophesied during the reigns of Uzziah (791–740 B.C.), Jotham (750–736 B.C.), Ahaz (736–716 B.C.), and Hezekiah

(716–687 B.C.). Isaiah received his revelation from God in a vision.

Corruption of Judah (1:2–9)

Invoking heaven and earth as witnesses (v. 2), the Lord announced His judgment of the nation. Even animals know their master but Israel does not know its Master (vv. 2–3). Because of sin and rebellion they have abandoned the Lord—they are like a body that is sick from head to toe (vv. 5–6). But sin has a price tag and payday is imminent. Isaiah envisions the desolation of the land caused by Sennacherib.

Sennacherib

Sennacherib was the Assyrian king who devastated the land of Judah in 701 B.C. (vv. 7–9).

Chastisement by the Lord (1:10–31)

Judah's apostasy was so severe that the Lord referred to them by the metaphors Sodom and Gomorrah (v. 10). They had offered the religious externals (sacrifices and celebration of the feast days), but the Lord simply saw it as a "trampling of my courts" (v. 12). The Lord used strong language—He *hated* their festival celebrations (festivals He had prescribed that they perform; Exod. 29; Lev. 1–7; 23; Num. 28) when they were done the wrong way—without a loyal heart. They were hypocritical: the hands held out in prayer were blood stained (v. 15).

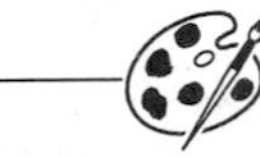

Survivors

Isaiah mentions "survivors" of the devastation by Sennacherib. This is the principle of a remnant that is found not only in Isaiah, but throughout Scripture (cp. 4:3; 6:13; 10:20–23; 11:11, 16; 17:6; 26:1; 28:5; 37:31; 65:9; Jer. 5:10, 18; Rom. 9:27; 11:5). Ultimately a remnant of Jews would be saved through the tribulation and enter Messiah's kingdom (Zech. 13:8–9).

In verses 16–20 the Lord gives the solution to the problem of their false worship (vv. 10–15). He exhorts them to do justice in the social realm: defending the orphan and the widow (v. 17; cp. 10:2; Pss. 68:5; 146:9; James 1:27). Using legal, courtroom terms, the Lord invites Judah to argue their case before Him (v. 18). If they return in obedience, though their sins are like scarlet (the color of sin; Num. 19:2, 6, 9), they will be white as snow—pure. Then God will bless them in the land (Deut. 16:20).

The Lord reminded Judah of the nature of her sin (vv. 21–23). She was like a harlot who was unfaithful to her husband (v. 21; cp. Hos. 1:2; 3:1). Her sins were enormous: murder, rebellion, theft, bribery. Instead of the purity of silver, she had become dross, the waste material, and diluted wine (v. 22). As a result, God would enter into judgment with Judah (v. 24f.), smelting away the dross—undoubtedly a symbol of the Babylonian captivity in 586 B.C. "Then" (v. 26) marks a transition, viewing the future messianic age when Israel indeed has repented and returned to the Lord in righteousness. Then He will bless the nation; Jerusalem will be called the "faithful city" (v. 26). In that future day Israel will be ashamed of her past idolatry (vv. 29–30).

It is possible to do the right thing the wrong way. It is right to attend worship services, witness, tithe, visit the sick, but these things can be done with the wrong motive. If the heart is wrong—if it is only an outward exhibition without a corresponding inner conviction and commitment—it is spiritually without value.

PREDICTION OF JUDGMENT AND BLESSING (2:1–6:13)

The twofold message of the prophet, judgment and blessing, is seen in the opening chapters. Chapter 1 described the sinful status of the nation; the end of the chapter viewed the nation's repentance with the resultant future blessing of the millennial kingdom (2:1–4).

The Future Judgment upon the Nation (2:1–4:6)

The "mountain" refers to Mt. Moriah, the Temple mount in Jerusalem, and it is prominent in Isaiah (cp. 11:9; 25:6–7; 27:13; 30:29; 56:7; 57:13; 65:11, 25; 66:20). This is where Solomon's Temple was built (1 Kings 6) and this is also where the millennial temple would be built (Ezek. 40–43).

Establishment of the Millennial Kingdom (2:1–4). These verses continue the thought of 1:26–31. Following their repentance, the nation will enjoy blessing in Messiah's kingdom. The "mountain" establishes the location of the future kingdom—Jerusalem located on Mt. Moriah. There will be topographical changes as Jerusalem is physically elevated (v. 2) to depict its supreme position in the world. The nations of the world will be subservient to Israel as the nations come to Israel to acknowledge its sovereignty (v. 2; 11:14–15; Zech. 14:16). Jerusalem will be both the political and spiritual headquarters in those days as God's truth is transmitted from Jerusalem (v. 3). The entire earth will experience peace when weapons of warfare will be used for peaceful purposes (v. 4).

The nation was guilty of adopting the heathen religion and morality of the pagan nations (v. 6, 9). In disobedience and distrust of the Lord, the nation amassed silver, gold, and horses—a violation of Deut. 17:15–17—because it revealed a lack of faith in the Lord.

Judgment in Preparation of the Millennial Kingdom (2:5–4:1). In view of the future glory of the millennial kingdom, the Lord admonished Judah concerning their present disobedience. Before the future blessing can come, the nation must deal with their present sin. The Lord delineated their sin in 2:5–9.

For their disobedience the nation would be judged 2:10–11. The fierce judgment anticipates the future tribulation when God would use the tribulation to bring His people Israel to repentance. The phrase "in that day" (v. 11) links this judgment with a distant future event (cp. 2:2, 17; Rev. 6:16).

Interpretation Insight
The prophet frequently blends the historical with the future prophetic. In 2:10–11 the prophet blends the historical judgments on Israel and Judah in the Assyrian (722 B.C.) and Babylonian (586 B.C.) captivities with the future judgment in the tribulation (Rev. 6–19).

The day of the Lord, describing the future tribulation judgment, expands to all the nations of the world (2:12–22). The "day of reckoning" is "that day" (vv. 17, 20) when Christ returns at His second advent to judge all humanity (v. 19, 21). The pride of people, illustrated by the lofty cedars of Lebanon and oaks of Bashan (v. 13) will particularly be judged (v. 17). The "mountains," "hills," and "high towers" (vv. 14–15) refer to Gentile kingdoms with their military might. Christ's return will result in their demise; the pride of nations will be humbled. Idols will be ineffective (v. 18); people will scramble into caves for refuge because of the Lord's return in judgment (v. 19; Rev. 6:15–16). Because of the Lord's impending judgment, Judah should stop trusting in human might and turn to the Lord in repentance (v. 22).

What can our society expect when the sin of homosexuality is openly paraded as an acceptable alternate lifestyle, even though God has pronounced judgment against it? Study Gen. 19:1–10; Lev. 18:22; 20:13; Rom. 1:26, 27; 1 Cor. 6:9; Gal. 5:19–21; Eph. 5:5; 1 Tim. 1:10; Jude 7.

The day of the Lord will be a time of judgment on Jerusalem and Judah (3:1–12). Their punishment is enunciated in verses 1–7. The staples of life—bread and water—will be removed. Four areas of deprivation are noted: material deprivation—removal of food supplies (v. 1); spiritual deprivation—removal of judge and prophet (v. 2); military deprivation—removal of military leaders (v. 3a); and economic deprivation—removal of craftsmen (v. 3b). Instead, capricious children, i.e., incompetent, fickle leaders will rule over them; leaders will be despised (vv. 6–7). Their sin, which precipitated the judgment, is detailed in verses 8–12. They openly rebelled against the Lord, displaying their sin like Sodom. But amid the judgment, the righteous need not fear; they will benefit from righteous living (v. 10).

Branch (4:2)

"Branch" refers to Jesus Christ, since He is a branch or sprout that comes from the line of David (cp. 11:1). It is also a messianic title (cp. Jer. 23:5; 33:15; Zech. 3:8; 6:12). "Fruit of the earth" is a related title, indicating Messiah is a branch sprouting from the human, Davidic line and bearing the fruit of believers among the Jewish people (cp. John 15:1).

The rulers will also be judged (3:13–15). The elders and princes, the religious and civil rulers have ransacked the righteous and plundered the poor. Openly they have committed social injustices. The women, too, will be judged (3:16–4:1).

Manifestation of Messiah's Presence (4:2–6). Since the church age is not in view in the Old Testament (cp. Eph. 3:5ff.; Col. 1:25–27), the prophet spanned the centuries to the future day when the Messiah will return, restore the repentant Jewish people (v. 4), and inaugurate the millennial kingdom. The pattern of these chapters follows the twofold ministry of the prophets: judgment and blessing.

It is possible to become discouraged when we look at events in our society and the world. Unrighteousness appears to prevail. Yet God will write the last chapter; God will consummate this age precisely according to His sovereign plan. In that day, righteousness will prevail.

The Present Judgment upon the Nation (5:1–30)

Parable of the Vineyard (5:1–7). Using the figure of a vineyard to depict the nation Israel, God is pictured as the vineyard's cultivator—He cared for the vineyard by planting the choicest vines on fertile ground, removing the stones, and placing a watchtower in the vineyard to protect it from animals and thieves, enabling it to produce the choicest grapes. He placed a winepress in the vineyard—because He expected a harvest of grapes (vv. 1–2).

The cultivator did everything He could to produce a rich harvest of grapes—God cared for Israel, bringing them into the Promised Land and defeating their enemies—He did everything necessary for the nation to produce a harvest of righteousness (vv. 3–4). What was the result? Worthless grapes. Unrighteousness. Idolatry. Immorality. As a result, the divine cultivator promised to destroy the vineyard—a reference to the Babylonian invasion of Judah and destruction of Israel in 586 B.C. (vv. 5–6; cp. 2 Kings 25:1–12).

Israel is pictured as a vineyard with the Lord as the cultivator (cp. Ps. 80; Jer. 12:10). Jesus told a similar parable, depicting Israel as a vineyard (Matt. 21:33–46), with a similar conclusion. The ultimate fruit that God sought in Israel was recognition of Messiah—but the nation rejected Him (Matt. 21:42). In John 15, Jesus identifies Himself as the true vine which produces true righteousness, in contrast to Israel (John 15:1).

Verse 7 is a summary statement of the parable. It identifies Israel as the vineyard and interprets the parable—the good grapes God looked for were justice and righteousness.

Pronouncement of the Verdict (5:8–23). The six woes expand and explain the "worthless grapes" of the parable (vv. 2, 4). They detail the sins of the unrighteous nation. "Woe" is a strong exclamation, a warning or threat of impending

Sheol

Sheol is frequently a broad term, referring to the place of the dead in general (Gen. 37:35; Ps. 16:10). Here, however, it begins to take on the meaning of hell (cp. Num. 16:30; Deut. 32:22; Ps. 9:17) and is virtually equivalent to the N.T. concept of gehenna (Matt. 5:22, 29, 30; 23:15, 33).

disaster. The first woe is leveled at the materialists (vv. 8–10). A second woe was leveled at the drunkards (vv. 11–12). These people were so addicted to wine that they began and ended their day by imbibing wine. They reveled in the drunken musical feasts, ignoring God's mighty acts on their behalf (v. 12). For this reason they would go into exile in Babylon, a symbol of doing down to "Sheol" (vv. 13–14). In captivity their pride would be abased—then they would recognize God's holiness (vv. 15–17).

The third woe judges the defiant (vv. 18–19). These people defied the Lord by blatantly indulging in sin as though pulling their idol on a cart with ropes. They were tied to sin and defied the Lord to judge them. The fourth woe is aimed at those guilty of moral perversion (v. 20). They substituted evil—idolatry, adultery, immorality, dishonesty, materialism—for good. The fifth woe judged those guilty of pride and self-sufficiency, thinking they could deliver themselves without God's help (v. 21). The sixth woe indicted the leaders, who instead of providing honest government were drunken revelers, depriving the people of justice (vv. 22–23).

The reference may initially refer to the Assyrian King Sennacherib's invasion of Judah in 701 B.C. (2 Kings 18:13ff.; Isa. 36–37), but may also refer to Nebuchadnezzar, king of Judah, in his threefold invasion in 605, 597, 586 B.C. (2 Kings 24–25). Despite its long journey from the Tigris-Euphrates region, the troops would be fresh, strengthened by God for Judah's judgment (vv. 27–30). Like ferocious lions, they would devastate Judah (v. 29).

Pronouncement of the Sentence (5:24–30). "Therefore" marks the resultant judgment because of their innumerable sins. Their sins revealed that they rejected and scorned the law of the Lord (v. 24). As a result, they would be devastated as a grass fire destroys the stubble. The Lord's hand—a symbol of His power—would be stretched out against them in judgment rather than against their enemies. God would use Gentile nations to execute His punishment on Israel. By an uplifted flag (cp. 11:10, 12; 13:2; 18:3; 49:22), God would summon the nations from afar to Israel.

- *God had uniquely blessed Israel: He brought them into the Promised Land, provided for them, and gave them victory over their enemies. Now God looked for the fruit of righteousness, but there was none. Instead the nation scorned God's word, indulging in every form of sin. As a result, God would judge them by bringing a pagan nation against them.*

QUESTIONS TO GUIDE YOUR STUDY

1. What are some of the evidences that Isaiah was written by a single author?
2. Under what kings of Judah did Isaiah prophesy?
3. What were the sins of Judah that were about to bring God's judgment?
4. In chapter 5, to what does God compare Jerusalem? In the New Testament, who used this same metaphor for Israel?
5. Who were the world powers that would be the agents of God's judgment against His people?

There is always a reason for judgment. Perhaps people who indulge in sin expect to get away with it; perhaps they think no one sees them; hence, there is nothing to fear. But in His righteousness God will—and must—judge sin. Those who scorn His mercy and lovingkindness will eventually be judged in an eternal hell (Matt. 25:31, 36).

The Commissioning of Isaiah (6:1–13)

Isaiah's Vision (6:1–4). At the time of Uzziah's (also called Azariah) death (739 B.C.), Isaiah received a vision of God. Although Uzziah was a good king, he was struck with leprosy ten years before his death for intruding into the priest's office (2 Chron. 26:16–20). The conditions of chapter 5 may describe that period of time (cp. 2 Kings 15:4); the vision of the Lord's holiness would be significant at that occasion. The terms "high" and "lifted up" emphasize the Lord's exaltation; the "train of his robe" is reminiscent of a king's robes. Smoke was normally

Seraphim

Seraphim, meaning "burning ones," are celestial beings, generally resembling human beings. Each having six wings, they are pictured above the throne of God (cp. Rev. 4:8). In humility they cover their faces and in respect they cover their feet before God. Their purpose is to praise the holiness and power of God (v. 3) and bring communication from heaven to earth (v. 6).

evident in the Lord's presence (Exod. 19:18; 1 Kings 8:10–11). The Lord is exalted and sits enthroned—monarch of heaven and earth. Since Isaiah had a difficult message, a vision of the Lord's holiness would give him boldness in denouncing the nation for their sins.

Isaiah's Confession (6:5–7). Upon seeing the sovereign Lord in His majestic holiness, Isaiah immediately sensed his own sinfulness and the sinfulness of the nation. The "woe" suggests Isaiah saw himself as lost, expecting to be judged for his sinfulness. In the presence of God where everything praised the Lord with pure lips, Isaiah recognized the uncleanness of his own lips. With a burning coal from the altar (perhaps the altar of burnt offering; Lev. 6:12), a seraphim touched Isaiah's lips, signifying his lips were purified. His sin was taken away; Isaiah was now prepared to preach a pure message (v. 7).

Because of their refusal to listen to the Lord's message, the people would experience God's judicial hardening, even as Pharaoh had experienced it (Exod. 4:21; 7:14). The people in Jesus' day were similarly hardened (Matt. 13:14–15; Mark 4:12; Luke 8:10; cp. Acts 28:26–27).

Isaiah's Commission (6:8–13). The Lord questioned Isaiah (the word *us* implies the Trinity; cp. Gen. 1:26), giving the prophet an opportunity to respond. Recognizing the nation's need for cleansing, Isaiah volunteered. But his mission would be a difficult one: God commissioned the prophet to preach to a people who would not respond to him. In fact, after listening to Isaiah the people's hardness would intensify.

Isaiah inquired how long he would have to preach this message of judgment. God instructed the prophet to proclaim the message until the "cities are devastated"—until the Babylonian Exile. At that time the cities would be destroyed and the people taken captive "far away" to Babylon (v. 12).

Isaiah died before the captivity, but he was to continue preaching the message of condemnation throughout his life. But the Lord also provided hope. Like a sprout from a stump, a remnant—a tenth of the people—would remain in the land. These were the poor people that Nebuchadnezzar allowed to stay.

- *In order to preach a message of judgment to the people of Judah, Isaiah first had a vision of God's holiness. Only then could he properly preach the message of condemnation. God cleansed Isaiah in preparation for his ministry while reminding the prophet that the people would be hardened and refuse to respond to his message. For that reason they would eventually be taken into captivity, but a remnant would remain in the land.*

THE PREDICTION OF MESSIAH'S RULE (7:1–12:6)

In these chapters Isaiah blended Israel's immediate deliverance from foreign nations with Israel's ultimate, future deliverance under Messiah. He will return in triumph, conquer the nations, and establish Israel in the millennial kingdom.

It is vital that we have a correct concept of God before we can properly serve Him in this world. We will never properly appreciate the sinfulness of humanity and the need for God's righteous judgment until we have a biblical perspective of God's holiness.

The Prediction of Messiah's Advent (7:1–25)

Confrontation of Israel and Syria (7:1–2). In 734 B.C. Pekah, king of Israel, and Rezin, king of Syria, formed an alliance in an attempt to protect themselves from the mighty Assyrian power. They sought to bring Judah into their alliance, threatening Ahaz with a replacement puppet king if he refused to cooperate. When Ahaz, king of Judah, heard that the Syrians and Israelites were camped in Ephraim (Israel's largest tribe, representing the entire nation of Israel) in preparation for war against him, he was terrified (v. 2).

Ephraim was Israel's largest tribe. Here it represented the entire nation.

Protection of the Lord (7:3–16). In preparation for the expected invasion, Ahaz was inspecting Judah's water supply when the Lord sent Isaiah

Shearjashub

Shearjashub, means "a remnant shall return."

This was historically fulfilled: In 722 B.C. the Assyrians took Israel captive into Assyria (2 Kings 17:24) and in 669 B.C.—sixty-five years after this prophecy—Ashurbanipal, king of Assyria (669–626), repopulated Israel with foreigners who intermarried with the remaining Israelites left in the land (which resulted in the Samaritan people).

Virgin

The Hebrew word *almah,* translated "virgin," means a young, unmarried woman; it is never used of a married woman. When Matthew quoted Isaiah 7:1 he used the Greek word *parthenos,* which clearly means "virgin" (Matt. 1:23). Conclusion: Isaiah 7:14 is a prophecy of the virgin birth of Christ.

and his son, Shearjashub, to meet King Ahaz (v. 3). Ahaz was faced with a problem: Should he go to Assyria for help or should he trust the Lord? Isaiah exhorted Ahaz to remain calm and unafraid. Israel and Syria were nothing more than "two stubs of smoldering firebrands"; like smoldering pieces of firewood, they would be burned up and vanish (v. 4). God would not permit the Syrian-Israel alliance to succeed (v. 7).

Why should Ahaz fear? Syria and Israel only had human leaders (vv. 8–9). In fact, in just sixty-five years Israel would cease to exist.

Since Ahaz refused to believe Isaiah, the Lord invited Ahaz to ask for a sign, but the pious king refused—out of fear. Since Ahaz was afraid to ask for a sign himself, the Lord would give him a sign—the sign of "Immanuel," "God with us" (v. 14). Three things would concern the prophecy of the child to be born: (1) He would be born of a virgin (v. 14); (2) He would be raised during a time of famine and suffering (v. 15); (3) He would still be a boy when the Syrian-Israel alliance would be destroyed (v. 16).

Differing views are held concerning the prophecy of the virgin. (1) The strictly messianic view recognizes Isaiah 7:14 only as a prophecy of the virgin birth of Christ. It is completely fulfilled in the virgin birth of Christ (Matt. 1:23). (2) The "double fulfillment" or "double reference" view sees a near fulfillment in the birth of Isaiah's son and a far fulfillment in the virgin birth of Christ. In the near prophecy, the woman was a virgin when the prophecy was given and later became Isaiah's second wife. She served as a type of Mary, and the son to be born was a type of Christ. By the time this child was twelve, the two nations whom Ahaz feared would be destroyed (vv. 15–16).

Assyria destroyed Syria in 732 B.C. and conquered Israel in 722 B.C.

Invasion by Assyria (7:17–25). The Assyrians would enter the land like stinging bees (v. 18), swarming everywhere in the land (v. 19). But in Judah the Assyrians would clash with the Egyptians (vv. 18–19), and as a result, the land would be devastated, as though shaved with a razor (vv. 17, 20).

Shaving the hair and beard was a symbol of humiliation (Job 1:20; Isa. 15:2; Jer. 47:5; 48:37; Ezek. 7:18; Amos 8:10; Mic. 1:16).

King Ahaz of Judah was fearful because of the Syrian-Israel coalition threatening him. Isaiah prophesied that within sixty-five years the nations that threatened him would be destroyed, verifying the promise with a sign—a virgin would conceive and bear a son. The prophecy would have an immediate fulfillment in the birth of Isaiah's son and a far fulfillment in the birth of Jesus Christ. However, in the meantime, Assyria would enter Judah and devastate the land.

Frequently when we are faced with a dilemma, we are tempted to seek a human way out of the problem. We may manipulate or seek erroneous resolutions instead of trusting the Lord. The Lord may put difficulties in our paths to determine the sincerity of our trust in Him.

The Prediction of the Future Invasion (8:1–9:7)

The Prediction of Mahershalalhashbaz (8:1–4). To visually remind the people of Syria's and Israel's destruction, Isaiah wrote the name of the yet unconceived child on a large scroll, "Mahershalalhashbaz." The boy's name would testify to the destruction of Syria and Israel. Two witnesses would confirm the truthfulness of Isaiah's prophecy. So Isaiah's new wife conceived and gave birth to a son, Mahershalalhashbaz, and before he was old enough to say "My father" or "My mother," Syria and Israel were destroyed in just two years hence—732 B.C.

"Mahershalalhashbaz" is the longest name in the Bible and means "swift is the booty, speedy is the prey."

Peoples

The "peoples" ("nations") in verse 9 symbolize the nations of the world that oppose Messiah and the Jewish people. At the end of the age, the nations of the world would be crushed for their opposition to Messiah and His people (cp. Ps. 2:1–5; Zech. 14:1–3; Rev. 19:15–21).

Hebrews 2:13 quotes Isaiah 8:17–18, indicating Isaiah and his children are types of Christ and His spiritual children.

Faith is frequently the issue. Our problem is not our circumstances, our finances, or our family. The issue is whether we will trust the Lord in a crisis. But where does trust—and faith—come from? We develop faith through reading the Word (Rom. 10:17). There is nothing more vital that we can do to develop our faith than reading the Scriptures.

The Prediction of Assyria's Invasion (8:5–8). But Syria and Israel would not be the only ones to feel the crush of the Assyrians. Since Judah had rejected the "gently flowing waters of Shiloah"—a figure of the Lord's gentle dealing with Judah, they would also experience the Assyrian invasion.

The Prediction of the Lord's Conquest of Assyria (8:9–15). Despite the impending Assyrian invasion of Judah, the Lord brought a word of encouragement. The nations (Assyria and Babylon) that would inflict punishment on Judah would themselves be punished.

The Exhortation to Trust the Lord (8:16–22). The Lord instructed Isaiah to seal up the testimony of Mahershalalhashbaz and wait for its fulfillment, despite the suffering in the land (vv. 16–17).

Because of the people's inclination to know the future and to seek it through pagan mediums and psychics, Isaiah exhorted them to seek knowledge from the living God rather than dead pagans (v. 19). The only trustworthy standard is the Word of God; hence, "to the law and to the testimony!" (v. 20).

Isaiah's son, Mahershalalhashbaz was a testimony that God would destroy Syria and Israel, Judah's enemies, within two years. But Assyria, the instrument of God's judgment, would also be felt in Judah by Sennacherib's invasion in 701 B.C. Nonetheless, Judah would be spared, but God was with them. So the people should trust the Lord, seeking truth and encouragement from His Word.

The Prediction of Messiah's Deliverance (9:1–7). Isaiah shifted to the future when the nation that had suffered because of foreign oppressors would be delivered and live in the glory of Messiah's presence. Zebulun and Naphthali are the tribal territories in Galilee that felt the devastation of Assyria's invasion in 743 B.C. and 734 and 732 B.C. (2 Kings 15:29) and were ultimately taken captive in 722 B.C. (2 Kings 17:6). "In earlier times" reflects the Assyrian invasions; "later on" looks to the future, to Messiah's advent (v. 1, NASB).

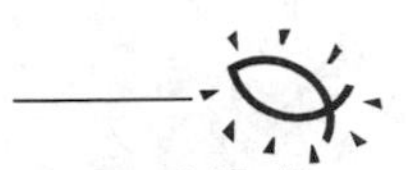

Matthew 4:15–16 indicates that when Christ settled in Capernaum, He fulfilled this promise by His presence in Galilee.

While verses 1b–3 envision Christ's first coming, verses 4–5 anticipate His second coming when He will break the yoke of foreign oppression (Zech. 12:3, 6, 9; 14:3). It will be similar to Gideon's conquest of Midian (Judg. 7:1–25). When Christ conquers the nations at His second coming, the implements of warfare will be destroyed (v. 5).

Messiah will be the "Wonderful Counselor," meaning He will be a supernatural counselor (Judg. 13:18) who brings the promise of eternal life (John 3:16). He is also the "Mighty God," a term used of the Lord (Deut. 10:17; Isa. 10:21; Jer. 32:18). He will be mighty in battle on behalf of Israel. Christ is the "eternal Father"—this does not mean He is God the Father; the persons of the Trinity are distinct. But Christ has the title of Father. The statement affirms His eternality and therefore His deity; it also says He is tender and faithful, a wise guardian and provider of His people. Christ is the "Prince of Peace," anticipating the glorious millennial kingdom when He brings peace to the earth (11:6–9; 65:17–25).

Isaiah described Messiah's advent in verses 5 and 6, again merging the first and second comings of Christ. He will be a child that is born, reflecting His humanity, and anticipating the virgin birth (7:14; Matt. 1:23), but He is also a Son, reflecting His deity—a Son that is destined to rule as the government of the world (Ps. 2:7–9; Mic. 5:2; Zech. 14:9). Christ's glorious rule will have no end (v. 7; Dan. 7:14, 27; Luke 1:33; Rev. 11:15).

Amid suffering, God's people may find great encouragement and hope because there is a glorious day coming when Christ will right all the wrongs and inaugurate His glorious kingdom wherein peace will reign. And we can have a foretaste of that today (John 14:27; 16:33).

The prophet looked into the future and saw a glorious day coming when the nation that had suffered oppression from foreign invaders like Assyria and Babylon would bask in the glorious blessing of the Messiah. The prophet intermingled the first and second comings of Christ; at the Second Coming, Christ will ultimately and finally break the yoke of Israel's bondage to foreign oppressors.

The Prediction of Samaria's Judgment (9:8–10:4)

The prophet returned to the historical circumstances of his day. He indicted the Northern Kingdom of Israel for their unrepentant hearts. Apparently they had not learned their lesson with the invasion of Tiglath-pileser in 734 B.C. For this reason God promised to raise up the Syrians under King Rezin, who would invade Israel from the east (v. 11), and the Philistines, who would attack from the west (v. 12). But in spite of the Lord's chastisement, the nation remained unrepentant (v. 13).

"Hand" or "arm" is a symbol of strength and may mean God's strength on behalf of Israel (Deut. 5:15) or against Israel in judgment as it is used here. God's outstretched hand in judgment against Israel would continue.

In 10:1–4 Isaiah detailed some specifics of their sins. The leaders were guilty of perverting justice, stealing from the widows and orphans (v. 2). But their ill-gotten wealth would not help them in the end. Punishment would not escape them (v. 3); God's hand would remain outstretched against them in judgment (v. 4).

In spite of God's chastisement against Israel through the Assyrian invasions, the nation remained unrepentant. The entire nation—from the prophet to the poor people—all were corrupt. For this reason God's hand would remain outstretched against them in judgment.

God speaks to us in the circumstances of life, but the question is, How do we listen? Do we hear God's voice? Do we learn from the events that happen in our lives or do they harden us? God desires a repentant and contrite heart in us (Ps. 51:17).

The Prediction of Assyria's Destruction (10:5–34)

Because Israel was a godless nation, the Lord sent Assyria against Israel in judgment. God used Assyria as the "rod of my anger" in taking His disobedient child, Israel, into the divine woodshed for divine discipline.

Because of Assyria's pride, when God completed His disciplinary action on His people Israel, He promised to punish Assyria (v. 12). Assyria's pride is detailed in verses 13–14.

Assyria is pictured as an axe and a saw with the Lord wielding the implements (v. 15). The one who uses a club or a rod has power over it. Because Assyria failed to recognize the Lord's sovereign purpose, He would send a disease among the Assyrian soldiers. The "light of Israel" would devour the Assyrian soldiers in a single day.

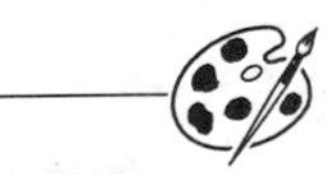

Lord of Hosts

"Lord of hosts" is a title of the Lord meaning "to wage war." It pictures the Lord as a victorious warrior surrounded by the heavenly armies in battle against Israel's enemies (1 Sam. 17:45; Ps. 24:10; 46:7, 11).

In verses 20–23 the prophet looked beyond Israel and Judah's captivities to the time of the return from captivity in Babylon.

Assyria's assault on Judah in 701 B.C. is detailed in verses 28–32. The Judeans were terrified as Sennacherib began his march toward Jerusalem, halting at Nob, within sight of the sacred city, Jerusalem. But God would stop them. The Assyrians are depicted as a lofty tree that is cut

There is an interplay between divine sovereignty and human responsibility. If God is God, then He must be sovereign and in control of all events. If He is not sovereign, then He is not God. Yet God's sovereignty does not vitiate man's responsibility. People are responsible for their actions. I am responsible for my actions. I can never attribute my sinful actions to God's sovereignty.

down, felled with a terrible crash, illustrative of the 185,000 Assyrians that were struck dead (37:36). Like a great cedar felled in the forest of Lebanon, the Lord brought down the mighty Assyrian army (v. 34).

Although Assyria was used by the Lord to discipline Israel, the pagan nation exceeded God's purpose, determining to destroy Israel. Because of Assyria's pride, God promised to destroy Assyria, a prophecy that was fulfilled when Babylon conquered Assyria in 612 B.C.

The Prediction of Messiah's Kingdom (11:1–12:6)

With the destruction of Assyria, representing Gentile hostility against Israel, the prophet envisioned the future day when Messiah would rule over Israel in the millennial kingdom. In that day Messiah will restore what Adam lost, bringing justice to the world and peace to the animal kingdom. The remnant of Israel will be restored and enjoy a preeminent position.

The Administration of Messiah (11:1–16). *The Lineage of Messiah (11:1).* The transition from chapter 11 is intentional. While Assyria will be cut down like a tree in the forest (10:33–34), a shoot will sprout from Jesse, the Davidic, kingly line (Matt. 1:1). Cutting down the Davidic tree was the Babylonian captivity; the sprouting of the stump is Messiah—He will restore Israel to a place of glory. Messiah, the Branch, will bear fruit; He will fulfill the promised Davidic Covenant (2 Sam. 7:16). As a descendent of David, Messiah will establish a kingdom and a rule that will endure forever (Dan. 2:44–45; 7:13–14).

The Justice in Messiah's Kingdom (11:2–5). Messiah will be supernaturally empowered by the Holy Spirit, who descended on Him at His baptism (Matt. 3:16–17; John 1:32–33). The attributes of the Spirit that rest on Christ are stated in three couplets of two; Messiah will exhibit wisdom and understanding, counsel and strength, knowledge and fear of the Lord (v. 2). Christ will rule as King over the earth, ruling with perfect justice.

The Peace in Messiah's Kingdom (11:6–9). The fall of man in the garden of Eden brought sin and chaos to the world (Gen. 3), but Messiah's rule will restore what Adam lost, including peace in the animal kingdom (Ps. 8:6–7). Seven animals are listed in couplets with those that are normally their prey. As someone has remarked, the leopard will lie down with the goat today but only the leopard will get up!

Because of the unconditional promises of the Abrahamic Covenant (Gen. 12:1–3; 15:12–21), the Davidic Covenant (2 Sam. 7:16), and the New Covenant (Jer. 31:31–34), Israel will enjoy a prominent place in Messiah's kingdom. But the Gentiles will also be blessed in Messiah's kingdom (Gen. 12:3; Isa. 2:2–4; 60:5–14; 66:18–21).

The Universal Acclaim of Messiah's Kingdom (11:10). Israel will be restored to the land and acknowledge the Messiah (Ezek. 36–37); the nations will show their allegiance to "Messiah's flag" (cp. Zech. 14:9, 16).

The Gathering of Israel into Messiah's Kingdom (11:11–16). The Hebrew people will be restored to the land of Israel a "second time"—the first restoration was from captivity in Babylon in 536 B.C. (Ezra 1–2). But this restoration will be greater—they will come from all over the earth, migrating to the land of Israel (vv. 11–12; cp. Ezek. 36:24; 37:12–14, 21). In that day Israel and Judah will no longer be divided; they will be united (v. 13). Moreover, they will defeat and dominate the nations of the world (v. 14). The Lord will dry up the gulf of the Red Sea and the

The Northern Kingdom of Israel was taken captive into Assyria in 722 B.C. and the Southern Kingdom of Judah was taken captive to Babylon by Nebuchadnezzar in 586 B.C. When Cyrus, king of Persia, decreed in 538 B.C. that Israel could return, a remnant of Israel and Judah returned under Zerubbabel in 536 B.C. (Ezra 1–2).

Euphrates River, paving the way for Israel's safe and glorious return to the land (vv. 15–16).

The Worship Accorded Messiah (12:1–6). Chapter 12 logically follows the focus of chapter 11. With the advent of Messiah and the establishment of the millennial kingdom (ch. 11), the Lord is worshiped (ch. 12). The worship on earth in the millennium is a counterpart of the heavenly worship pictured in Rev. 5:13; 15:3–4 during the tribulation. The prophecies concerning Judah (chaps. 1–12) have come to an end in chapter 12. They began with chastisement and the announcement of judgment, but they have ended with Israel's blessing in Messiah's kingdom.

A descendant of David, son of Jesse, will arise—the Messiah will come to Israel in the power of the Holy Spirit. He will reign as King in righteousness over the Israelites who have returned to the land from around the world. All the nations of the world will be subject to Messiah—even nature itself will be restored. Messiah will be worshiped in the millennial kingdom.

Someone has said that we would get along better in this world if we recognized that we live in a fallen world. But there is a day coming when Christ will return, establish justice and righteousness in this world. When we are disappointed over the injustices in this world, we should remind ourselves that there is a day coming when genuine righteousness will prevail.

QUESTIONS TO GUIDE YOUR STUDY

1. Describe Isaiah's call to be a prophet.
2. What nations did Ahaz fear? What did Isaiah tell Ahaz regarding those nations?
3. What sign did Isaiah bring from the Lord to Ahaz? In what two ways was the sign fulfilled?
4. What are the characteristics of Messiah?
5. What did God do when Assyria went beyond the role God intended them to play with respect to Israel?

Prophecies Concerning the Nations (13:1–23:18)

These chapters parallel Jeremiah 46–51 and Ezekiel 25–32.

A transition occurs in chapter 13. While chapters 1–12 deal with judgments on Judah and Jerusalem, chapters 13–23 broaden the focus of God's judgment to include the Gentile nations. The reasons for the prophecies of judgment on the Gentile nations are: (1) to preserve Israel from despair when Gentile nations oppress them; (2) to prevent Israel from forming an alliance with the nations; (3) to predict the eventual downfall of all Gentile powers; (4) to produce faith in Israel; and (5) to proclaim Messiah's authority over all earthly Gentile powers.

JUDGMENT OF BABYLON (13:1–14:23)

Since Babylon was the empire that destroyed Jerusalem and took the people of Judah captive in 586 B.C., it is purposeful that Babylon heads the list of Gentile nations that God will judge.

Although Babylon was a historic nation, it also symbolized Gentile opposition to the Lord. From the tower of Babel (Gen. 10:10) to "Babylon the Great, the mother of prostitutes" (Rev. 17:5), Babylon epitomizes Gentile rebellion against God. And God will judge the rebel Gentile nations.

Destruction of Babylon (13:1–22)

Arrival of the Enemy (13:1–5). Isaiah delivered an "oracle," a weighty, burdensome message of judgment against Babylon (v. 1). The invaders come from "a faraway land"—Persia, which lay 350 miles east of Babylon—to destroy the proud Babylonians (v. 5).

Anticipation of the Greater Babylon (13:6–13). The term "day of the Lord" can refer to any judgment by the Lord, historically or prophetically. It appears the prophet again blended the historic judgment of Babylon with the future judgment of Babylon in the last days. The passage begins with a description of the people's fear at the Medo-Persian invasion in 539 B.C. (vv. 6–8) but transitions to the future day at the end of the

Day of the Lord

"Day of the Lord" may be used in three ways: (1) it may characterize any judgment of God in history (e.g., the Babylonian destruction by the Medo-Persians in 539 B.C.); (2) it may refer to an eschatological judgment at the end of the age (vv. 9–13; Joel 2:31); (3) it may denote blessings of the millennial kingdom (Joel 3:18; Zeph. 3:15).

age when prophetic Babylon will be destroyed (vv. 9–13; Rev. 14:8).

Administration of Judgment by the Medes (13:14–22). When the Medo-Persians invade, the Babylonians will be like hunted gazelles and sheep—ready prey for the hunters (vv. 14–15).

Restoration of Israel (14:1–32)

This chapter logically builds on the preceding. When the Gentile powers are ultimately destroyed, then God will bring Israel into peace and rest in the millennial kingdom.

Prediction of Israel's Restoration (14:1–3). In that future day, God will "again choose Israel," bringing them back into the land, giving them rest and peace from their enemies (Ezek. 36–37).

Annihilation of Israel's Enemy (14:4–17). The prophet composes a taunt song in celebration of the anticipated destruction of the Babylonian tyrant.

Interpretation Insight

Differing views are held concerning verses 12–17: (1) it refers only to the king of Babylon; (2) it refers to Satan, the real power behind the king of Babylon; (3) it refers to Satan's fall from his position of preeminence before God, either pre-Edenic or between Genesis 2 and 3.

Destruction of Babylon (14:18–23). These verses return to a discussion of the king of Babylon and his destruction in 539 B.C. In ancient times an unburied corpse was a calamity and a curse—the greatest of insults (cp. 1 Sam. 31:9–13). Babylon's king (probably a reference to Belshazzar) will not receive a royal burial, not even a pauper's funeral—his corpse will be trampled underfoot and cast on the ground like a dead branch (v. 19; cp. Dan. 5:30). His children would not succeed him on the throne (vv. 20–22) and the land of his rule would become desolate (v. 23).

Satan is a "schemer" (Eph. 6:11) both on the personal and national level. He seeks to devour (1 Pet. 5:8); he also determines to destroy God's people Israel. On a personal level God calls us to resist him by standing firm in our faith (1 Pet. 5:9) and taking on the full armor of God (Eph. 6:10–18).

- *Babylon, the epitome of Gentile rebellion against God, will ultimately be destroyed. Historically, it occurred when the Medo-Persians conquered Babylon in 539 B.C.; prophetically, it will occur toward the end of the tribulation period (Rev. 17–18).*

JUDGMENT OF ASSYRIA (14:24–27)

To illustrate the certainty of God's judgment on Babylon, Isaiah compares the certainty of Babylon's demise to the defeat of Sennacherib in 701 B.C. in which 185,000 Assyrians were killed (37:36).

JUDGMENT OF PHILISTIA (14:28–32)

The Philistines, who had recently seized four Judean cities (2 Chron. 28:18), rejoiced over King Ahaz's death. Their joy, however, would be shortlived. A "viper" (Hezekiah) would come from the serpent's root (Ahaz), indicating Hezekiah would defeat the Philistines (2 Kings 18:8).

Moab, lying east of the southern end of the Dead Sea, was an enemy of Israel. They attempted to place a curse on Israel (Num. 22–24); their women seduced the Israelite men (Num. 31:15–17); under Eglon they oppressed Israel for eighteen years (Judg. 3:12–14). There were endless wars between Moab and Israel (1 Sam. 14:47; 2 Sam. 8:2, 12; 2 Kings 3:5–27).

JUDGMENT OF MOAB (15:1–16:14)

The Devastation of Moab (15:1–9)

Isaiah delivered the oracle, the weighty, burdensome message, concerning Moab in which its major cities were destroyed. Ar and Kir, likely located near the southern end of the Dead Sea, had already been destroyed in Isaiah's day.

The Expectation of Moab (16:1–5)

For security the Moabites fled southward some fifty miles to Sela in Edom; like young birds thrown from their nest, the women sought to cross the shallow part of the Arnon River. But real security would only be found in Israel, the daughter of Zion—anticipating Jerusalem would not be destroyed in Assyria's invasion in 701 B.C. (cp. 10:24–34; 37:36–38). Moab could obtain this security with a tribute payment to Judah (cp. 2 Kings 3:4). So Moab sought refuge in Judah (vv. 3–4). Here the prophet seems to span the centuries into the eschatological future. Ultimate rescue will come from a descendant of David, the Messiah—He will rule in justice and righteousness (vv. 4–5; cp. 9:7; 11:4; 28:6; 32:16; 33:5; 42:1, 3, 4; 51:5).

The Explanation of Moab's Fall (16:6–12)

Pride is the reason for God's judgment of Moab (v. 6). For this reason the raisin cake delicacies will be absent; grainfields, vineyards, and orchards will wither (vv. 8–10).

The Destruction of Moab (16:13–14)

The precise date of this prophecy and fulfillment is uncertain. One view is that the prophecy was given in 704 B.C. Sennacherib, the Assyrian invader, passed southward through Judah and on to Moab in 701 B.C., fulfilling the prophecy in that year. An alternate view is that the prophecy is given in 734 B.C. and fulfilled by Tiglath-pileser three years later. Still another view suggests this was fulfilled by King Sargon of Assyria in 715 B.C.

- *The prophet delivered the burdensome message that Moab will be destroyed by the Assyrian army, resulting in devastation of the land. The people will cry in horror and flee south to their ally, Edom.*
- *Pride is the reason God will judge Moab.*

Somehow sins seem to have a way of catching up with us. Sins that seem long forgotten, when they are not resolved, surface again. In fact, we eventually have to resolve our sins with the very people with whom we had difficulties—just like Moab with Israel. Repentance, seeking restoration, and forgiveness is always the right way (Eph. 4:32; Col. 3:13; 1 John 1:9).

JUDGMENT OF DAMASCUS (17:1–14)

The Prediction of Damascus's Destruction (17:1–3)

This chapter is probably contemporaneous with Isaiah 7. Damascus, the capital city of Syria, the nation that had allied itself with the Northern Kingdom of Israel against Assyria, would become a heap of ruins (v. 1). This prophecy was fulfilled in 732 B.C.

The Rescue of the Remnant (17:4–11)

"In that day" suggests Isaiah again looked to the prophetic future and transitioned his thought to Israel at the end of the age. The event is the future tribulation period when "the glory of Jacob will fade"—Israel will suffer in the tribulation (v. 4). But a remnant of Israel will be left (a common theme in Isaiah; see "Word Picture" on 1:8).

The Agent of Destruction (17:12–14)

The focus turns back to the Assyrian invasion of Judah in 701 B.C. The mighty Assyrian army roared like the sea and rushed onward like turbulent water in the invasion. But suddenly the invaders were turned back. God stopped the Assyrians and spared Jerusalem (vv. 13–14; 37:36–38).

Geographically, ancient Cush represented what today is southern Egypt, Sudan, and northern Ethiopia. Politically, Cush may refer to the Twenty-Fifth Dynasty of Ethiopia that established itself in Egypt under Piankhi; his son is called "So" in 2 Kings 17:4.

Snaking through the Sudan and Egypt for four thousand miles, the Nile River is the longest in the world. The lifeblood of Egypt, the Nile was worshiped as the Egyptian deity, Hapi. Constant equatorial rains supplied abundant water. In ancient Egypt (before the construction of modern dams), the Nile overflowed its banks from June through October, then receded. During January through March the fields would dry and bear bumper crops. There were three seasons: inundation (June-October), planting (October-February), and harvest (February-June).

JUDGMENT OF ETHIOPIA (18:1–7)

"Alas" is an expression of humiliation, signifying compassion because the mighty Egypt-Ethiopian empire will be conquered by the mightier Assyria (cp. 17:12). Because Egypt-Ethiopia encouraged Israel and Judah to defy the Assyrians, Assyria extended its tentacles by invading Egypt-Ethiopia.

JUDGMENT OF EGYPT (19:1–20:6)

The people of Judah looked to Egypt for help against the mighty Assyrians. God warned them that Egypt would not help them (cp. Ezek. 17:1–21).

Affliction Through Civil War (19:1–4)

In bringing a burdensome message concerning Egypt, Isaiah pictured the Lord riding on a cloud, coming in judgment against Egypt (v. 1). The picture reflects an impending civil war, apparently referring to the Twenty-Third Libyan Dynasty clashing with the Ethiopians (v. 2).

Affliction Through Drought (19:5–10)

God's judgment promised to bring a drought on Egypt, with the mighty Nile and its tributaries drying up, creating a stench throughout Egypt (vv. 5–6). Fishermen would no longer ply their trade (v. 8); the garment industry would suffer because water was needed to grow flax, which was used in manufacturing linen (v. 9). Egypt's economy would be destroyed.

Confusion of Wise Men (19:11–15)

Although known for its wise men and priding itself for its learning and wisdom (1 Kings 4:30), in the day of judgment Egypt's wisdom would fail.

Conversion of Egypt (19:16–25)

"In that day" (vv. 16, 18, 19, 21, 23, 24) indicates Isaiah was looking to the future, with a prophecy concerning the end of the age. The Assyrian judgment of Egypt will prefigure the Christ's judgment of Egypt at His Second Coming. In that day, because Israel will be converted (Zech. 12:10–14), the land of Judah will be preeminent in the world, creating fear in Egypt (v. 17). Egypt will be subject to Israel in that day, even learning Hebrew in going to Israel to worship (v. 18; cp. Zech. 14:16–19).

"City of Destruction" may read "City of the Sun," referring to Heliopolis, a center for worshiping the sun god. It would be destroyed. In that day Egypt will worship Israel's God, with an altar in the center of Egypt and a pillar near the border (v. 19), as a sign of Egypt's faith in the Lord (v. 20). The Egyptians will be converted to a true faith in Israel's Messiah (v. 21). Then the Lord will listen to their prayers; Christ will become their Savior and champion (v. 20). In this millennial picture, Egypt will worship the Lord with memorial sacrifices (v. 21; cp. Zech. 14:16–19; Mal. 1:11).

Even the Assyrians will be subject to Israel's Messiah in that day, worshiping the Messiah alongside the Egyptians (v. 23). In that day Israel will be an intermediary between Egypt and Assyria, with a highway linking two former enemies (v. 24). In the millennium, these three former enemies will live in harmony (v. 25).

Prediction Concerning Egypt (20:1–6)

In 711 B.C. Sargon II, king of Assyria, captured Ashdod, a Philistine city. This event was a warning to the people of Judah who sought an alliance with Egypt against Assyria: Egypt would also be crushed under the Assyrian onslaught. As an object lesson, Isaiah removed his outer garment and sandals. Even as Isaiah walked around naked and barefoot, so the people of Egypt and Cush—young and old alike—would suffer humiliation and impoverishment by the invading Assyrians (v. 4). (The Assyrians would strip the entire clothing from their captives.) As a result, the people of Judah who sought an alliance with Egypt would be ashamed (v. 5), realizing their hope in Egypt had been in vain (v. 6). They should have trusted the Lord.

Wearing only his undergarment in public would have been a great humiliation, being considered "naked" (vv. 2–3). Walking barefoot was a further picture of humility without protection against the stony ground. Isaiah was a sign against Cush (ch. 18) and Egypt (ch. 19).

Self-reliance can be a dangerous thing. As the Egyptians trusted in their wisdom and the resources of the Nile River, so believers can be fooled into trusting in their education, job, health, or finances. But all of these will fail. Our trust and confidence should be in the Lord (Prov. 3:5–6).

The Medo-Persian Empire was an alliance of the Medes and the Persians (Elam was an ancient name for Persia, referring to the land east of Babylon, beyond the Euphrates River). In 612 B.C. the Medes helped the Chaldeans (Babylonians) capture Nineveh and destroy the Assyrian empire. In 549 B.C. Cyrus the Great of Persia subdued the Medes, giving birth to the Medo-Persian Empire (cp. Esth. 1:19; Dan. 5:28). In 539 B.C. Cyrus conquered the mighty Babylonian Empire.

God promised to judge Egypt through civil war and by bringing drought to the nation that relied on the Nile River. Their wise men would not cope with God's judgment. But in the future millennial kingdom, Egypt would be converted, acknowledging Israel's Messiah and living in peace with Israel and Assyria.

JUDGMENT OF BABYLON (21:1–10)

Babylon's Destruction (21:1–4)

The "Desert by the Sea" describes the Babylonian plain by the Tigris and Euphrates rivers. The object of this oracle is identified as Babylon (v. 9). The invading Persians and Medes would come against Babylon like a storm across the desert (vv. 1–2). In 546 B.C. the Elamites attacked southern Babylon and in 539 B.C. the alliance of Medes and Persians conquered Babylon. As Isaiah foresaw the impending disaster, he was filled with horror (vv. 3–4).

Isaiah's Observation (21:5–9)

In a vision Isaiah foresaw the reckless, sinful banqueting of Belshazzar (Dan. 5) but on that very night in 539 B.C. Belshazzar was killed and the Babylonian kingdom conquered (Dan. 5:30). God instructed Isaiah to post a watchman on the city wall, to look for the eastern invaders (v. 6). When the sentry saw the invading forces (v. 7), he would cry out, warning the city of the impending attack (v. 8). Suddenly the invasion came and a man cried out, "Babylon has fallen, has fallen" (v. 9). The words are reminiscent of Rev. 14:8 and 18:2. Isaiah might have been blending the historic with the prophetic, anticipating eschatological Babylon's fall at the end of the age.

Edom was the land south of the Dead Sea. Edom means "red," signifying the red sandstone of the Edomite desert. Seir means "hairy" and refers to the rugged mountain range rising to 5,600 feet in Edom. Seir is used as a synonym for Edom. This was the land given to Esau and his descendants (Gen. 32:3; Josh. 24:4).

The Jews' Liberation (21:10)

But Babylon's defeat would mean the Hebrews' liberation. The people that had been "threshed"—afflicted—would be set free.

JUDGMENT OF EDOM (21:11–12)

The questioner from Seir asked how long Edom would continue to suffer. The watchman informed him that deliverance for Israel was coming, but Edom would continue to suffer. "If you would ask, then ask; and come back yet again" seems to invite repentance (v. 12).

JUDGMENT OF ARABIA (21:13–17)

This oracle announced that the Assyrians would also inflict punishment on the Arab tribes of the desert. In a year, Kedar's splendor (they were known for their beautiful tents) would be destroyed. Assyria's domination of the Arabian tribes began in 732 B.C., with Sargon II invading them in 726 and 715 B.C.

Dedanites are the descendants of Abraham and Keturah (Gen. 25:3; 1 Chron. 1:32) who settled in Edom (others suggest on the Persian Gulf). Tema was an oasis on the Arabian peninsula, 250 miles southeast of Aqaba (cp. Job 6:19; Jer. 25:23). Kedar was located south of Israel and east of Egypt (Gen. 25:18). These people were nomadic (Ps. 120:5; Song 1:5).

JUDGMENT OF JERUSALEM (22:1–25)

Having dealt with the nations surrounding Jerusalem, Isaiah now turned his attention to God's judgment on Jerusalem.

Devastation of Jerusalem (22:1–14)

Because Jerusalem was surrounded by valleys on three sides, this oracle is addressed to "the Valley of Vision." Isaiah described the Babylonian invasion and siege against Jerusalem led by Nebuchadnezzar in 588–586 B.C. (2 Kings 25). Jerusalem is boisterous because people from the surrounding towns and villages have sought refuge in the walled city (v. 2). But the city is captured as King Zedekiah flees (2 Kings 25:5) and the inhabitants are taken captive to Babylon (v. 3; 2 Kings 25:6–11).

Isaiah was beyond comfort as he wept profusely over the city's destruction (v. 4). It is a day of panic as the walls of Jerusalem are torn down (2 Kings 25:4). Troops from Elam (Persia) and Kir (an Aramean city), now allied with Babylon, take up the assault (v. 6). The Kidron Valley is filled with chariots in their attack on Jerusalem (v. 7), breaching the walls (v. 9). The people of Jerusalem attempt to preserve their water supply and shore up the broken walls, but to no avail; they have failed to trust the Lord (v. 11). The resolution to Jerusalem's dilemma was repentance—God called them to weep in repentance and to exhibit their repentance by shaving their heads and putting on sackcloth (v. 12). Instead, they engaged in revelry. The people had the pagan philosophy, "Eat and drink, . . . for tomorrow we die" (v. 13). But their sin would not be forgiven (v. 14).

Description of Two Rulers (22:15–25)

In an earlier event, the Lord specifically indicted Shebna, a government official who apparently was second only to the king (cp. 36:3; 2 Kings 15:5). Shebna was pro-Egyptian, and he sought an alliance with Egypt from Hezekiah (cp. chaps. 30–31). Shebna would be replaced by Eliakim, a trusted man who would care for the people in Judah (vv. 20–21).

Judah and Jerusalem, like the surrounding pagan neighbor nations, would also be judged. The Babylonians would attack the city and break down her walls. In spite of Judah's every effort, they would not sustain a defence—because they failed to trust the Lord. God's solution was repentance, but the people of Judah rejoiced in revelry instead.

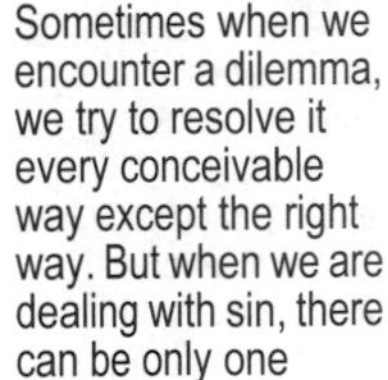

Sometimes when we encounter a dilemma, we try to resolve it every conceivable way except the right way. But when we are dealing with sin, there can be only one resolution (1 John 1:9). If we attempt to hide our sin, there will be no resolution (Prov. 28:13).

JUDGMENT OF TYRE (23:1–18)

Destruction of Tyre (23:1–14)

Trading ships were harbored at Cyprus, northwest of Tyre, when they heard of Tyre's conquest. Isaiah called on the traders to wail because Tyre's lucrative trading business was destroyed.

What happened? Who planned the destruction of this wealthy city with its renowned traders (v. 8)? The Lord of hosts. He was responsible for judging this city of pride. Isaiah instructed the people of Tarshish to lament because the Lord had demolished Tyre's trading commerce. He would stretch out His hand in judgment against Tyre (v. 11).

Tyre had established itself as a world class trader, the "queen of the seas," with its phenomenal harbor. Its merchants traded far and wide, establishing numerous colonies. The city was in two parts, one on the mainland, and the other on a protected island one-half mile from shore. Nebuchadnezzar captured the mainland city in 572 B.C., and Alexander finally conquered the island city in 332 B.C. by building a causeway to the city and besieging it—a venture that lasted seven months.

Restoration of Tyre (23:15–18)

In 701 B.C. Assyria established Tyre as a vassal city, restricting its trade. The seventy years would be from 700 to 630 B.C. when Assyria declined in power, enabling Tyre to establish its trade once more. Like a forgotten prostitute, Tyre would again ply her trade, singing to entice her lovers (v. 16). This time, however, the profits from her trade would benefit the Lord's people (v. 18).

Personal fortune is never a source of security. A downturn in the economy, ill health, bankruptcy, or disaster can quickly wipe out personal fortune. The Lord is our only genuine security.

Tyre, the great commercial trading enterprise that had established itself throughout the Mediterranean world, from Egypt to Spain, would be destroyed by the Lord because of its pride. Alexander the Great brought this prophecy to fulfillment in 332 B.C., when he destroyed the city.

QUESTIONS TO GUIDE YOUR STUDY

1. What does Babylon symbolize?
2. Why did God judge Moab?
3. In what two ways would God judge Egypt?
4. What world power would God use to judge Jerusalem?
5. What leader brought to fulfillment Isaiah's prophecy concerning Tyre?

PROPHECIES OF UNIVERSAL JUDGMENT AND MILLENNIAL BLESSING (24:1–27:13)

Like the finale that brings the music together in a grand crescendo, these chapters create an explosive conclusion in judgment. Having begun with prophecies of judgment on Jerusalem and Judah (Isa. 1–12), and the judgment of the nations (Isa. 13–23), the judgments now expand to include the judgment of the world at the end of the age. These chapters detail the Lord's judgment on the earth during the tribulation (Rev. 6–19). They are Isaiah's version of the apocalypse.

ESTABLISHMENT OF THE MILLENNIAL KINGDOM (24:1–23)

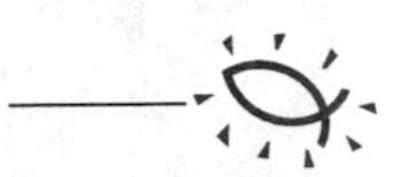

The judgment described in this chapter parallels Matt. 24 and Rev. 6–19.

Chaos of the World (24:1–13)

"Behold" always anticipates a future event. The prophet declared the universality of judgment—the *earth* will be judged (vv. 1, 3, 4, 5, 6). The universality of this judgment will not only be reflected in nations, but also individuals. Judgment will fall on all classes. There will be no class distinction. Priest and people, servant and master, maid and mistress, buyer and seller—all will be judged (v. 2). The earth will be laid waste and plundered. Judgment comes because God's people have violated His laws and broken His covenant (v. 5).

Praise of the Remnant (24:14–16)

All over the earth, from the west (v. 14), to the east, and to the islands of the sea (v. 15), the godly remnant that survives the tribulation will praise the Lord for His righteous judgments (cp. Rev. 7:1–10; 15:3–4; 16:5, 7; 19:2). As Isaiah reflected on the people of his day, he cried out, pronouncing a woe on himself as he saw the sinfulness around him.

Judgment of the World (24:17–23)

Escape from God's worldwide judgment will be impossible. If the people escape one terror, another will befall them (v. 18).

In that day God will punish "the host of heaven." Satan and his emissaries will be judged, as well as the earthly rulers (Rev. 19:20; 20:1–3, 10).

BLESSINGS OF THE MILLENNIAL KINGDOM (25:1–12)

In chapter 25 and most of chapter 26 the godly remnant sings a song of praise to the Lord in the millennium following the tribulation. The millennium is pictured as a banquet where Gentiles from around the world will come to Jerusalem to acknowledge Christ's kingdom rule on earth (v. 6). In Scripture, mountains frequently denote governmental rule (cp. Dan. 2:44–45); "this mountain" is Jerusalem, the seat of Christ's millennial rule.

Above all else, God is to be worshiped. Perhaps we are weak and negligent in worship. But worship is essential. If we recognize God's greatness, His faithfulness in delivering us from dilemmas of life, we must respond in worship. The Lord is a great God and worthy of our worship.

- *God will climax this world's history with a judgment of the entire world. The nations that scorned God's name and God's truth will be judged at the return of Christ. At that time Christ will receive the praise of the godly remnant who live through the tribulation as He establishes the millennial kingdom on earth.*

WORSHIP IN THE MILLENNIAL KINGDOM (26:1–27:13)

Song of Praise to the Lord (26:1–21)

Praise for Rescue (26:1–4). "In that day" (26:1; 27:1) identifies the occasion as the messianic reign of Christ. As the millennial kingdom is inaugurated, the remnant of Israel sings praises to the Lord for His protection. The godly enter the gates of Jerusalem, but their security is the Lord (vv. 1–2). Instead of physical walls, salvation will be their wall of protection. Because they trusted in the Lord, they enjoy peace—both physical and spiritual peace in the kingdom because Messiah reigns (v. 3; Ps. 112:7–8).

Gentiles worshiping God in the tribulation is a common theme. Gentiles will come to Jerusalem to worship and learn God's truth—the city where Christ is King (Isa. 2:2–3). Then Gentiles will have a knowledge of God (Isa. 11:9) and keep His word (Isa. 56:6). The nations that refuse to worship in Jerusalem will suffer deprivation (Zech. 14:17–19). God's name will be honored through the Gentile nations (Mal. 1:11).

Praise for Judgment of Enemies (26:5–11). Those who trusted in the lofty city (25:12) will be brought low; Israel's enemies will be destroyed (v. 5).

Praise for Permanent Victory over Enemies (26:12–15). The remnant praises the Lord, confessing that they served Him alone even when they were dominated by others (v. 13). He has brought them into the land, fulfilling the promises to the patriarchs, blessing them in the land (Gen. 12:1–3; 13:14–18; 15:18; 26:2–4).

Praise for Rescue from Suffering (26:16–21). Pictured as a pregnant woman giving birth, Israel could barely whisper a prayer during the time of suffering. Isaiah is picturing Israel's suffering during the tribulation (Jer. 30:7; Matt. 24:9). But following the tribulation, there is hope of the resurrection (v. 19).

PRAISE FOR THE PRESERVATION OF ISRAEL (27:1–13)

From Her Enemies (27:1–6). "In that day" (see 26:1), Israel's enemies, portrayed by the slithering serpent, will ultimately be destroyed by the Lord (v. 1). At the end of the tribulation, God will rescue Israel and destroy its enemies. But Israel will blossom like a fruitful vineyard in the millennial kingdom (v. 2). (This song of the vineyard is contrasted with 5:1–7.)

Peace may be outward and inward. Isaiah pictured the day when Christ will return to establish physical peace in the world. There will be complete peace in that day—no wars, no crime, no violence of any kind. However, believers will also enjoy spiritual peace at all times. Jesus promised us "His" peace (John 14:27). During outward tribulation we may still have inner peace (John 16:33).

From Its Trials (27:7–13). In order for Israel to bear fruit, God had to discipline the disobedient nation. But the Lord did not punish Israel the same way He punished Israel's enemies (v. 7); He would chasten them by the "east wind" (v. 8). He would bring the Babylonians, like a hot desert wind, against Israel, taking them into captivity in Babylon, where they would be purified (vv. 8–9; Deut. 28:49–52, 64; 2 Kings 17:23; 25:1–12). This was fulfilled in 586 B.C. when Jerusalem's inhabitants were carried into captivity in Babylon (v. 10; 2 Kings 25:1–12).

There is great value in living righteously. The momentary suffering or difficulties are just that—momentary (Rom. 8:18). God will bring us into a "level" place; He will smooth the path for us so we may live in peace. The key is trust. Amid trials we may still enjoy peace (Isa. 26:3; John 14:27; 16:33).

But "in that day" when the Lord rescues a repentant nation, He will judge the nations that have oppressed Israel—from "the flowing Euphrates" (Babylon) to "the Wadi of Egypt" (Egypt) (v. 12). Israel will be regathered from the nations and restored to the land (v. 13; Matt. 24:31). Believing Israel will be regathered to "the holy mountain," Mount Zion in Jerusalem where Jesus Christ will reign as King in the millennium.

"In that day," at the time of Christ's return to earth, He will rescue the repentant remnant of Israel and restore them to the land. But He will judge the Gentile nations that have afflicted Israel. Then Israel will rejoice and sing praises to the Lord for His protection.

PROPHECIES CONCERNING APOSTATE ISRAEL AND JUDAH (28:1–33:24)

In these chapters Isaiah pronounced five woes on those who scorn God's word. He principally indicted Israel and Judah for failing to trust God; they trusted their wealth instead and sought help through foreign alliances.

WOE AGAINST THE DRUNKARDS AND SCOFFERS (28:1–29)

Corruption of Ephraim (28:1–4)

The first woe is levelled at Ephraim, the large tribe that was representative of the Northern Kingdom of Israel. This prophecy was given prior to the fall of the Northern Kingdom in 722 B.C. and anticipated the Assyrian invasion.

Ephraim is termed "the pride of the drunkards" (vv. 1, 3), alluding to Samaria, built on a hill (1 Kings 16:24) with a command of the lush, surrounding countryside where drunkenness was rampant. Samaria was the capital of the Northern Kingdom but also the seat of idolatry (1 Kings 16:32–33; Isa. 9:9; Jer. 23:13; Ezek. 16:46–55; Amos 6:1).

Coronation of the Remnant (28:5–6)

"In that day" indicates Isaiah looked to the future, the end of the age, when the remnant of Israel would repent and receive a glorious diadem—the Lord Himself when He inaugurates the millennium on His return (v. 5).

Corruption of Israel (28:7–13)

The prophet returned to describe the conditions of his day: The people are enslaved to wine. Even the prophets and priests are drunkards, attempting to render spiritual decisions while drunk (v. 7). Their banquet tables are filled with their vomit (v. 8). And the priests and prophets ridiculed Isaiah for treating them like children that had just been weaned (v. 9), suggesting he was speaking baby talk to them (v. 10).

Because of their stubborn refusal to respond to God's word spoken through the prophet, God announced He would speak to them in a foreign tongue—the Assyrian language.

Warning to Judah (28:14–22)

The lesson of what happened to the Northern Kingdom of Israel was a lesson to the Southern Kingdom of Judah. Like their northern neighbors, they were also guilty of scoffing at Isaiah's words (v. 14), of failing to trust the Lord (v. 16), and of sin (v. 17). The Lord indicted the leaders in Jerusalem who had made a covenant with "death," likely a reference to Egypt (20:6; 29:15; 30:1–2; 31:1).

In 701 B.C. Sennacherib, leading the Assyrian army, would trample Judah, destroying forty-six towns and villages (vv. 18–19). In metaphorical language, Isaiah reminded them "the

The Scriptures use numerous metaphors. In this section, "death" and "Sheol" are metaphors for Egypt—symbolic of Judah's failed foreign alliance (v. 15). "Cornerstone" is a metaphor for Christ, the firm foundation for believers (v. 16; 1 Cor. 3:11). "The bed is too short" and "the blanket too narrow" picture inadequacy—the failed foreign alliances. Their resources will fail.

When we are being disciplined by the Lord, it is an unpleasant experience. Yet the very fact that God deals with us is a sign of our sonship. If we weren't His children, He wouldn't bother with us (Heb. 12:6–8). Amid the discipline, we must learn to endure (Heb. 12:2–3) and we must learn the lessons He wants us to learn (Heb. 12:10).

bed is too short" and "the blanket [is] too narrow"—their resources would fail (v. 20).

Encouragement to the Remnant in Judah (28:23–29)

The prophet also had a word of comfort for the godly remnant in Judah (vv. 23–29). God's disciplinary judgment of Judah will not continue forever (v. 23). Just as a farmer does not continually plow and harrow the ground, so God will not continue to plow Judah in judgment (v. 24).

The prideful, drunken people of Israel would experience God's judgment through the Assyrian invasion, which would take the Northern Kingdom captive to Assyria in 722 B.C. But the Southern Kingdom of Judah was no better. They would also feel God's discipline through Sennacherib's invasion in 701 B.C. Yet God's just discipline would not last forever; it would come to an end.

WOE AGAINST JERUSALEM (29:1–14)

Siege Against Jerusalem (29:1–8)

The prophet lamented as he pronounced a woe on the city where David once lived (2 Sam. 5:7–9). God promised to bring His judgment of fire on Jerusalem. Sennacherib, leading the Assyrian army, would encircle the city, humiliating it (vv. 3–4). In their fear, the people of Jerusalem would only speak in whispers (v. 4).

But Sennacherib would not conquer Jerusalem. Jerusalem's enemy would suddenly be blown away, like dust and chaff. Amid the Assyrian assault on Jerusalem, the angel of the Lord struck 185,000 Assyrians during the night

(v. 5). In the morning, when Sennacherib saw what had happened, the Assyrian army ceased their assault on Jerusalem and returned home (37:36–37). Those nations that wage war against Jerusalem will be like a dream, a vision (v. 7). They will disappear. Nations that hungered and thirsted for Jerusalem's destruction will fail. The language suggests Isaiah was looking beyond his time. At the end of the age, when the nations assault Jerusalem, the Lord Himself will fight against those nations and destroy them (Zech. 14:2–3; Rev. 19:15).

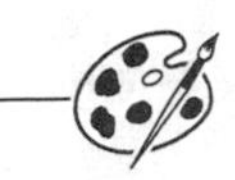

Ariel

"Ariel, the city where David once camped" (29:1, NASB) refers to Jerusalem. Some suggest "Ariel" means "lion of God," but that is probably incorrect. "Ariel" likely means "altar hearth" (Ezek. 43:15–16), hence, "fire," suggesting God's fire of judgment on Judah (Isa. 31:9). Here the fire refers to Sennacherib's fiery invasion in 701 B.C.

Spiritual Failure of Jerusalem (29:9–14)

The prophet resumed the Lord's condemnation of Judah for its sins. The nation had blinded itself (v. 9), hence, the Lord also blinded it (v. 10; cp. Rom. 11:25).

WOE AGAINST THE SCHEMERS (29:15–24)

In their depravity, these evil schemers attempted to hide their plans from the Lord, thinking He did not see them. They were foolish, thinking the potter is not greater than the clay, thinking God has no understanding (v. 16).

WOE AGAINST THOSE TRUSTING IN EGYPT (30:1–33)

With the threat of the Assyrians under Sennacherib on their doorstep, Judah sought help through an alliance with Egypt, a waning power, instead of trusting the Lord.

Admonition Against the Alliance (30:1–5)

A third woe is pronounced on Judah for their rebellion against the Lord—they were trusting in Egypt rather than the Lord. But Judah's hope in Egypt was doomed to failure; they would be put to shame (vv. 3, 5).

God is just. This is an important attribute of God. It means that God is entirely right in all His dealings with humanity. And His dealings are in relation to His standard and His word. The justice of God demands that He reward the obedient and punish the disobedient (Ps. 99:4; Isa. 3:10, 11; Rom. 1:32; 2:6; Rom. 6:23; 1 Pet. 1:17).

Teacher

"Teacher" is a title of Messiah. In the millennium, the Messiah will teach the people the way of truth and they will walk in it (2:3; 30:20). Jesus revealed His messiahship through His teaching. When He finished teaching the Sermon on the Mount, the people recognized His unique, authoritative teaching (Matt. 7:28–29). The four Gospels give approximately half of their writing to the words of Christ, reflecting His authoritative teaching.

Prediction of the Failure of the Alliance (30:6–17)

The prophet announced his burdensome message against Egypt—"the animals of the Negev." The Judeans sent donkeys and camels, loaded with gifts to pay for Egypt's help, travelling through the snake-infested desert; yet it was all in vain (vv. 6–7). Egypt was like Rahab, the mythical female sea monster (perhaps the hippopotamus) who did nothing (v. 7). Egypt would be of no help to Judah.

Restoration of Israel (30:18–26)

Verse 18 marks a transition as Isaiah looked to the distant day when Judah's discipline would be removed. The Lord longs to be gracious and compassionate to Judah but because He is just, He cannot condone sin. Sin must be dealt with. But a future day is coming when the people of Jerusalem will no longer weep. The Teacher—Messiah—will be among them (v. 20). He will teach them the way of truth and they will walk in it (v. 21; 2:3). No longer will they condone idolatry (v. 22).

Destruction of Assyria (30:27–33)

This section explains what must happen before Israel will be blessed in the land during the millennium: Israel's enemies must be destroyed. The judgment of the nations is just and will be meted out with the music of tambourines and lyres (v. 32). Topheth, the place where the pagan god Molech was worshiped, will be judged (v. 33).

Instead of trusting the Lord, Judah sought a military alliance with Egypt because of Assyria's threat. However, the alliance would fail and Judah would be chastened. When the chastening was over, God would destroy Israel's enemies, the nations of the world, and bring Israel into the millennial blessings under Messiah's rule.

The political correctness and tolerance agenda creates enormous harm to the Christian message. Political correctness and tolerance disallow speaking against any other view. Every view is acceptable. This places a great burden and dilemma on the Christian. We can never compromise the true gospel. We cannot condone or tolerate false views.

WOE AGAINST THOSE TRUSTING IN MILITARY DEFENSE (31:1–32:20)

Deliverance from Israel's Enemy (31:1–9)

The fourth woe continues the theme of condemnation against Judah for looking to Egypt for military help against the invading Assyrians. They rely on Egypt's military strength—their horses and chariots—instead of trusting in the Lord, who alone is able to deliver them. This was both unbelief and disobedience (Deut. 17:16).

Because the Lord promised to protect Judah, the people are called to return to Him and reject their idolatry (vv. 6–7). The Lord protected Jerusalem by sparing the city without a battle. During the night, the angel of the Lord killed 185,000 Assyrians, so the remaining army returned to Assyria (vv. 8–9; 37:36–38; 2 Kings 19:35). The Assyrians had been defeated by God, not man; by a divine sword, not a human one (v. 8). The fire of God's judgment would destroy the Assyrians (v. 9).

Return

"Return" is the same root word in Hebrew (shub) as "repent" (31:6). When a person repents, he returns to the Lord. It means to return to the Lord in obedience (Deut. 30:2). It is a call for Israel to turn from idolatry and evil and return to the Lord (Ezek. 14:6). The verb is frequently used among the prophets, calling for the covenant nation Israel to return to her God (Isa. 44:22; 55:7; 57:17; 59:20). This is different from the N.T. word "repent" *(metnoeo)* which means "change of mind" (Matt. 3:2; Acts 2:38). The N.T. distinction is seen in Acts 3:19.

Deliverance Through Messiah's Power (32:1–8)

Since the Lord will protect and deliver Jerusalem, Isaiah looked to the future millennium, when Christ would rule in righteousness as King (11:1–5; 33:17, 22; 44:6; 2:2–4; 9:3–7) and godly princes would rule under Him (Rev. 5:10; 20:6; 22:5).

Destruction of Worldly Society (32:9–14)

Isaiah returned to a denunciation of the people of his day, indicting the complacent women who were unmoved by Assyria's threat (vv. 9–10; cp. 3:16–21). Their complacency was ill-advised since the Assyrians would make their presence felt within a year. Then these complacent women would no longer drink wine and gather fruit (v. 10). Instead of complacency, they ought to have repented by putting on sackcloth (v. 11).

Description of the Spirit's Outpouring (32:15–20)

The prophet envisioned a future day, when following Jerusalem's destruction, the city and the land would again know peace. It will come when "the Spirit is poured out" (v. 15). Although the Spirit was poured out at Pentecost (Acts 2), Isaiah referred to Israel's future reception of the Spirit at the end of the tribulation (44:3; Ezek. 36:25–27; Joel 2:28–32).

- *Judah looked to a military alliance with Egypt to protect Jerusalem, but God said it would fail. Assyria destroyed the Judean towns and villages in 701 B.C., but the Lord promised to protect Jerusalem—and He did. The Assyrians returned home after the Lord destroyed 185,000. The Lord's promised protection anticipated the future millennium when Christ will reign as King, when Israel will respond to Messiah's teaching and enjoy His protective peace.*

Believers live both in the present and in the future. While we are responsible for our behavior in the present, we also look to the future, where we are promised that we will live and reign with Christ (2 Tim. 2:12; Rev. 22:5).

WOE AGAINST ASSYRIA (33:1–24)

The fifth and final woe is pronounced on Assyria, Judah's invader.

Destruction of Assyria (33:1–12)

The fifth woe is against Assyria, the "destroyer" and "traitor" (v. 1), perhaps so labeled because after having received the tribute money from Hezekiah, Sennacherib still demanded unconditional surrender (2 Kings 18:14–36). But the Lord would be victorious over Assyria. After Assyria finished Sennacherib's destructive work, he would be destroyed. The remnant of Judah appeal to the Lord for help (vv. 2–4). They know that the nations flee when the Lord speaks in judgment (v. 3); moreover, the plunder that Assyria has seized will become plunder for others (v. 4). Rejoicing in the Lord's omnipotence, the righteous praise God for His exaltation, for filling Jerusalem with justice and righteousness, with wisdom and knowledge, characteristics of the Messiah (vv. 5–6; 11:2; 9:6).

The historical background to Isaiah 33 is 2 Kings 18:14–36. Upon invading Judah in 701 B.C., Sennacherib received tribute payments of three hundred talents of silver and thirty talents of gold from King Hezekiah. But despite the tribute payments, the Assyrians demanded unconditional surrender from Judah. This was treachery.

But in the present there was no peace, only lamentation (vv. 7–9). Despite Hezekiah's tribute payment, there was no peace (2 Kings 18:14–17); the Assyrians still launched an invasion against Jerusalem. As a result of Assyria's treachery, the roads were deserted because of fear of the Assyrians; trade was inhibited, harming Judah's economy (v. 8). The land would suffer because of Assyria's destructive invasion (v. 9). "Now" marks the turning point (note the three occurrences of "now"). The Lord will respond to the faith and prayers of the remnant. He will merely blow on the Assyrians and they will burn up like chaff or stubble (vv. 10–12).

Lebanon is the coastal area north of Israel with its splendid cedar forests. Sharon is the fertile coastal plain south of Mount Carmel. Bashan (meaning "fertile plain") was the fruitful agricultural land east of the Sea of Galilee. Carmel (meaning "fruitful garden") was a fertile ridge extending twenty miles from the Mediterranean Sea into the Jezreel Valley.

Salvation of the Righteous (33:13–24)

In view of God's almighty power, people far away (Assyria) and near (Judah) must recognize what God has done. Sinners shake in fear. Who can live in the presence of a holy God who consumes the godless in fiery judgment (v. 14)? Those who live righteously, speaking the truth, rejecting dishonest business dealings, and avoiding evil (v. 15)—these will live securely and have abundant provisions (v. 16).

In anticipating the Lord's abundant blessings, Isaiah looked to the millennial age when the righteous would see the Messiah, the King in His beauty (v. 17). When He reigns, there will be no need for a national treasurer ("the one who took the revenue") or a defense secretary ("officer in charge of the towers") (v. 18). Foreign enemy nations with a strange language, like Assyria, will no longer terrorize them (v. 19). Never again will Jerusalem be destroyed; it will be undisturbed, a city of peace (v. 20). Enemy ships will run aground; Jerusalem will be protected with a moat (v. 21). In that future, millennial day, Messiah will be Israel's judge, lawgiver, and king. He will rescue Israel (v. 22)! The foreign ships will be looted—even the lame will plunder the foreign ships (v. 23). And the nation will be whole, physically and spiritually, because they are a forgiven people (v. 24; 35:5–6; Ezek. 36:25–32).

Our modern society appears to have lost its fear of God. George Burns played God in a Hollywood movie. A Los Angeles writer says God pouts when He can't get His way. An evangelical theologian writes that God's power is limited. Is it any wonder that the fear and reverence for God is gone? But that is not the biblical concept. Those who understand His greatness will revere Him (Isa. 6:1–5; 33:14; Prov. 1:7; Job 28:28). And those who obey Him will fellowship with Him (Ps. 24:3–4).

The Assyrians, under Sennacherib, subjugated Judah, forcing them to pay annual tribute while demanding their unconditional surrender. But the Lord, among whom only the righteous can live, would destroy the Assyrians. In the future millennial age, enemy nations will never again harm Israel. The righteous will live in peace with the Messiah.

Prophecies of Judgment and Blessing (34:1–35:10)

These chapters climax the subject of judgment and blessing which began in chapter 1. They reflect the common prophetic message in miniature: God pronounces judgment because of sin; upon the people's repentance He promises blessing, culminating in the millennial kingdom. Chapters 34–35 are to chapters 28–33 what chapters 24–27 are to chapters 13–23: Eschatological judgment is followed by millennial blessings.

DESTRUCTION OF THE GENTILE WORLD POWER (34:1–17)

Description of the Battle (34:1–7)

The judgment of Assyria (ch. 33) expands to the judgment of the Gentile nations of the world at the end of the age. "Nations," "people," "earth," and "world" identify this as universal judgment (v. 1). The description is of the final battle, the battle of Armageddon (Rev. 19:11–21).

Desolation Following the Battle (34:8–15)

Verse 8 is key—it explains the reason for the judgment—it is because of God's people Israel. The nations that persecuted Israel will be judged (v. 8; Joel 3:1–2; Zech. 14:1–4; Matt. 25:45–46). The land of Edom—representative of the nations—will burn and never be quenched (vv. 9–10; cp. Rev. 19:3). The land will be desolate, inhabited only by wild birds and animals (v. 11, 13–15). Its buildings will lie desolate, overgrown with weeds (v. 13). This will also be the fate of the nations that ignore the Lord and persecute His people.

Confirmation of the Prophecies (34:16–17)

After these things have transpired, people will consult the Scriptures and recognize that God's prophecies concerning these things have come true (cp. Matt. 5:18). All the animals that the Lord predicted will be there, each with its mate. The land will belong to them.

We can rely on all the promises, prophecies, and prohibitions, recognizing each one will come true. We can rejoice in the promises, anticipate the prophecies, and heed the prohibitions. God's Word will never fail. We can trust it implicitly.

BLESSING IN THE MILLENNIAL KINGDOM (35:1–10)

The prophecy switches from focusing on the destruction of Gentile world powers to the millennial blessings that will come to Israel. This chapter elaborates 33:17–24, contrasting the barrenness of Edom with the blossoming of Israel.

Restoration of the Land (35:1–2)

With the advent of Jesus the Messiah, the entire land will be transformed. Metaphorically, the barren desert is pictured as rejoicing because it will become lush land with blossoming flowers.

***Restoration of Physical Health* (35:3–6)**
In that millennial age the Lord will restore the sick. The weak will be strong; the fearful will be courageous; the blind will see and the deaf will hear. The crippled will leap like a deer and the mute will speak. Messiah's blessings, illustrated by the streams in the desert, will flow forth to all people in the millennial kingdom.

All the miracles of Jesus were messianic signs. He proved that He is the Messiah by performing the works of Messiah. When John the Baptist's messengers asked Jesus if He was the Messiah, Jesus simply answered by pointing to His miracles: the blind were seeing, the lame were walking, and the lepers were being cleansed (Matt. 11:5).

***Restoration of Spiritual Life* (35:7–10)**
The messianic kingdom will be a "highway of holiness." Only believers will enter the millennial kingdom (v. 8; 33:14–15; Ps. 24:3–4; Ezek. 20:38). Those who have been redeemed, those who have been ransomed by the blood of Christ, will live in Messiah's kingdom, amid everlasting joy.

The two common themes of judgment and blessing are reflected in chapters 34–35. Assyria and Edom reflect Christ's judgment on the Gentile world powers at the end of the age. The rebellious Gentile nations will be destroyed, never again to harass Israel. Then, at the Second Coming of Christ, there will be physical and spiritual changes. The desert regions will produce abundant vegetation and people will be healed of physical sufferings—foreshadowed by Christ's miracles when He was on earth. But only the godly will enjoy the millennial blessings. Only believers will enter the messianic kingdom.

There is a glorious future awaiting believers in the millennial kingdom. All earthly wrongs will be righted. Sufferings will cease. Maladies will be removed. But only believers will partake of these blessings. If you are not a believer, this present, fallen world is the only kingdom you will ever know, but if you put your trust in Jesus Christ as your sin bearer you also will have a glorious future to anticipate.

Historical Interlude (36:1–39:8)

Chapters 36–37 look back to chapters 1–35. They detail the historical background to the Assyrian invasion of Judah in 701 B.C. (Isa. 36:2–38:8 parallels 2 Kings 18:17–20:11.) God had promised to discipline Judah for its disobedience, using Assyria as His rod of chastisement; however, God also promised to spare Jerusalem and ultimately deliver Judah from Assyria.

Chapters 38–39 look ahead to chapters 40–66. They explain Hezekiah's request for God to lengthen his life. During that time he disobeyed by showing the visiting Chaldeans the treasures of Jerusalem. Nebuchadnezzar would later use that knowledge to invade Judah, destroy Jerusalem, and take the people captive to Babylon. Chapters 40–66 have Babylon as a focus.

INVASION OF SENNACHERIB (36:1–22)

Taunts of the Assyrians (36:1–10)

In 701 B.C., the fourteenth year of Hezekiah's reign (715–686 B.C.), Sennacherib, king of Assyria, invaded Judah, destroying forty-six towns and villages (according to his own record). With the invasion came taunting and intimidation. Sennacherib sent Rabshakeh (a title, not a name) to Hezekiah in Jerusalem, demanding the Judean king surrender to Assyria. Ironically, Hezekiah faced this challenge to his faith in the same location that the Syrian-Israel alliance had challenged Ahaz (v. 2; 7:3). But the God who delivered Ahaz would also deliver Hezekiah and Jerusalem! Eliakim, Shebna, and Joah were Hezekiah's negotiators who came out to meet the Assyrians (v. 3).

Aramaic was a Syrian language which had become the language of diplomacy, replacing Akkadian, which was Rabshakeh's native language. Although Aramaic was similar to Hebrew, the common people would not have understood it. They would only be conversant in Hebrew.

Intimidations of the Assyrians (36:11–22)

The Judean delegates asked Rabshakeh to speak to them in Aramaic, the Syrian language, which the common people of Judea—who were listening—would not understand (v. 11). The reason was obvious. The Judean leaders didn't want the Assyrian's intimidating words to strike fear into the Judean populace. But Rabshakeh understood the significance, and he continued to speak in Hebrew (probably through an interpreter) so all the Judeans would understand and fear the Assyrians (v. 12). To further intimidate the Judean people, Rabshakeh cried out in Hebrew with a loud voice, warning them not to listen to Hezekiah, who encouraged the people to trust in the Lord (vv. 14–15). He warned them to come out, surrender unconditionally, and he would take them to Assyria, a prosperous land (vv. 16–17). He warned them against thinking the Lord could deliver them—no one had ever escaped from the Assyrians (v. 18). The Syrian and Mesopotamian gods had not delivered them. Why should the Judeans think the Lord would deliver them? (vv. 19–20).

But the Judean delegates refused to answer the Assyrian; instead, they brought the somber message to Hezekiah (vv. 21–22).

Tearing one's clothes (usually a six-inch tear in the garment) signified grief and mourning over a calamity (Gen. 37:29; Josh. 7:6; 2 Kings 11:14; 19:1; 22:11; Esth. 4:1; Job 1:20; 2:12).

Sometimes our circumstances taunt and terrorize us. We look at our situation and there doesn't seem to be a good resolution. It doesn't add up. We look at alternative solutions and find none. But the enemy attempts to blind our eyes. The resolution is to walk by faith and not sight, trusting the Lord to deliver us from difficult circumstances (Heb. 11:1, 6).

The Assyrians had destroyed the Judean towns and villages and had surrounded Jerusalem, demanding unconditional surrender. They taunted the Judeans, suggesting neither Egypt nor the Lord was able to rescue them from the Assyrians.

CONSULTATION WITH ISAIAH (37:1–38)

Summoning of Isaiah (37:1–7)

In repentance and grief, Hezekiah tore his clothes and entered the temple—a sign that he was trusting the Lord to rescue the Judeans from the Assyrians. Hezekiah considered God's glorious name to have been insulted and profaned by the pagan nation. So he sent word to Isaiah, imploring the prophet to pray for the remnant in Judah (v. 4). Isaiah assured Hezekiah that God would indeed answer their petition. The Lord had heard the Assyrian's blasphemous speech and would cause him to return home, where Sennacherib would be assassinated (vv. 6–7; cp. vv. 36–38).

The nations that Assyria conquered were these: Gozan, a city of northeast Mesopotamia, was on the Habor River, a tributary of the Euphrates. Haran was a city in Syria, on the busy caravan road leading to Nineveh and Babylon. Rezeph was located near Haran, west of the Euphrates. Eden was on the Euphrates River north of the Balikh River. Telassar, meaning "hill of Asshur," was in upper Mesopotamia. Hamath was the capital of upper Syria in the Orontes valley. Arpad was twenty-five miles north of Aleppo and associated with Hamath. Sepharvaim was probably Sippar, southwest of Baghdad. Hena and Ivvah are unknown.

Warning of Rabshakeh (37:8–13)

Sennacherib was fighting against Lachish, a Judean town about thirty miles southwest of Jerusalem, when Rabshakeh came to report to him. Assyria momentarily shifted its strategy against Tirhakah, king of Cush (Ethiopia) (v. 9). But Sennacherib sent word to Hezekiah, warning the king not to trust in God to protect Jerusalem (v. 10). Sennacherib reminded Hezekiah of Assyria's conquests (v. 11); the gods of those nations did not deliver them and neither would the Lord deliver Jerusalem (vv. 12–13).

Request of Hezekiah (37:14–20)

Hezekiah took the threatening Assyrian letter, went into the Temple, and spread it out before the Lord, visually showing the Lord the letter. Then Hezekiah prayed a prayer of praise and confident trust in Almighty God. He praised God as being the "Lord of hosts," i.e., the God of the armies; He was the God of Israel, His people; and He alone, as Creator of heaven and earth, was God of all the earth's kingdoms—including Assyria (v. 16). On this exalting note, Hezekiah petitioned the Lord to hear the blasphemous words of Sennacherib and to see the Assyrian destruction of the countries (vv. 17–18). Hezekiah's purpose was that all the nations of the world would recognize the Lord, the only true God (v. 20).

Prediction of Isaiah (37:21–38)

Hezekiah prayed to the Lord, and the Lord immediately answered through Isaiah. The prophet brought Hezekiah the Lord's response (vv. 22–29). In response to Hezekiah's prayer, the people of Jerusalem ("daughter of Zion," "daughter of Jerusalem") would mock and ridicule the Assyrians. The pagan nation had blasphemed the Holy One of Israel (v. 23)! By mocking the people of Jerusalem, they had mocked the Lord (v. 24). The Assyrians were filled with pride, conquering countries as though by their own power (vv. 24–25), not recognizing the sovereignty of the Lord in all events (v. 26). For that reason Assyria's enemies were powerless to stop them (v. 27). God's knowledge was infinite. He was aware of the Assyrian arrogance. For that reason the Lord would take the Assyrians by a hook in the nose and lead in disgrace like a wild animal back to its home (vv. 28–29).

Because the Assyrians had devastated the countryside, the next two years would be difficult; but in the third year, they would sow and reap crops as in normal times. Judah would continue as a nation, with the remnant again prospering in the land (vv. 30–32). The Lord promised that Sennacherib would return to Assyria and would not enter or capture Jerusalem (vv. 33–34). The Lord was defending the sacred city (v. 35).

That night the angel of the Lord slew one hundred and eighty-five thousand Assyrian soldiers. When Sennacherib saw the destruction the next day, he returned home to Nineveh, where his two sons assassinated him (vv. 36–38).

- *When confronted by the Assyrians, the godly King Hezekiah summoned Isaiah for help. The Assyrians warned Hezekiah not to trust the Lord to deliver them, but instead Hezekiah showed the Lord the Assyrian's blasphemous threat and prayed in confidence to the sovereign Lord. Because of Hezekiah's trust, the Lord promised to protect Jerusalem and deliver the remnant. That night the Lord destroyed 185,000 Assyrian soldiers. Sennacherib returned to Assyria.*

The great British preacher, W. Graham Scroggie, once said, "He is at peace, whose God is sovereign." The concept we have of God will determine how we live. The question is not whether we will encounter difficulties in life. We will. How we respond to them is the key. If we recognize that God is sovereign over all events, over all people; that He controls everything, then we will enjoy His peace (cp. Eph. 1:11).

CONCLUSION OF HEZEKIAH'S REIGN (38:1–39:8)

Chronologically, chapters 38–39 precede chapters 36–37, but they are placed after chapters 36–37 because they anticipate the Babylonian captivity, the subject of chapters 40–66.

Hezekiah's Illness (38:1–8)

These verses parallel 2 Kings 20:1–11 in describing Hezekiah's illness. Since Hezekiah died in 686 B.C., and since God extended his life by fifteen years (v. 5), his illness was in 701 B.C., but before Sennacherib's invasion. When Hezekiah became ill, the Lord warned Hezekiah to prepare for his death (v. 1). When the king prayed, reminding the Lord of his faithfulness to Him, the Lord sent word through Isaiah that Hezekiah's life would be extended by fifteen years (v. 5). The Lord also promised to protect

Jerusalem from Assyria (v. 6). Moreover, the Lord promised to give Hezekiah a sign that his life would be lengthened: God promised to make the shadow on the stairway go back ten steps (v. 8). And it did.

The sign was an actual miracle wherein the Lord caused the sun's rays to go back ten steps on the stairway. It is not stated how the Lord performed this miracle. Since the Babylonians came to inquire about it, it apparently had not occurred in Babylon (2 Chron. 32:31). Therefore, it was a geographically localized miracle, restricted to the king's courtyard.

Hezekiah's Lament (38:9–20)

Hezekiah recorded his lament after he recovered from his illness. Hezekiah lamented his seemingly early death. In the middle of his life he would enter Sheol—the place where dead people went (v. 10). No longer would Hezekiah enjoy God's blessing in this earthly life, or fellowship with other people (v. 11). In picturesque language, Hezekiah saw his death as a shepherd's tent that is pulled up, as a piece of fabric is rolled up in a bolt of cloth (v. 12). Hezekiah felt as if God was a lion, breaking all his bones (v. 13). His pain made him twitter like a bird and moan like a dove (v. 14). But Hezekiah recognized God had spoken to him in his illness (v. 15).

Comforted that the Lord had restored his life, Hezekiah acknowledged that the illness was for his good (vv. 16–17). Not only did God restore his health, but the Lord also forgave Hezekiah's sins (v. 17). Hezekiah concluded with a vow of praise to God for his life, realizing that in death it is no longer possible to praise the Lord physically (vv. 18–20).

The Babylonians eventually destroyed the Assyrian empire in 612 B.C. and followed that with three successive invasions against Judah, in 605, 597, and 586 B.C. In Babylon's final assault, Jerusalem was captured, plundered, and burned. All the wealth of Jerusalem was taken to Babylon along with most of the people of Judah. In 539 B.C. the Medo-Persians conquered Babylon and Cyrus issued a decree permitting the people to return to Judah.

Hezekiah's Recovery (38:21–22)

A poultice of figs was used in medicinal treatment in the ancient Near East. God answered the prayer of Hezekiah and healed him, extending his life another fifteen years. The sign (v. 22) was given earlier (v. 8).

Hezekiah's Foolishness (39:1–4)

Having heard of Hezekiah's recovery, Merodach-baladan, king of Babylon, sent a congratulatory message and gifts to Hezekiah. The Judean king foolishly unveiled the Temple treasures to the pagan leaders (v. 3). All the grandeur of Solomon's Temple, covered with gold and silver, was shown to the Babylonians—an act that would bring disastrous consequences.

Isaiah's Prophecy (39:5–8)

Because of Hezekiah's foolishness in showing the Babylonians the Temple treasures, Isaiah announced that all those treasures would one day be plundered and carried away to Babylon (v. 6). Moreover, not only the treasures but also the people, royal descendants from Hezekiah himself, would be carried captive to Babylon (v. 7). The prophecy was literally fulfilled in 586 B.C. (2 Kings 25:1–12). Recognizing that he would enjoy peace during his own days, Hezekiah acknowledged the goodness of the prophecy.

- *When Hezekiah got sick, he prayed to the Lord, requesting that his life be spared. The Lord answered his prayer, extending his life fifteen years. But when the Babylonians heard of Hezekiah's recovery, they sent messengers whom Hezekiah received and showed all the Temple treasures. For his foolishness Isaiah announced the Babylonians would return, destroy and plunder the Temple, and carry the people captive to Babylon—a prophecy that was fulfilled in 586 B.C.*

God is sovereign in all His ways and in His infinite wisdom, He does what is best for us. We can make foolish requests and foolish decisions that are not best for us. Health and life are wonderful, but God has ordered our days. Our times are in His hands. We should submit to His sovereign will and rest in that, knowing that what God does is best.

QUESTIONS TO GUIDE YOUR STUDY

1. What is the reason for the judgments described in chapter 24?
2. What is Leviathan and what does it symbolize?
3. When Isaiah (31:8, NASB) declared, "The Assyrian will fall by a sword not of man," to what was he referring?
4. What did Hezekiah do when he received the threatening letter from Assyria?
5. What was Hezekiah's response on learning of his imminent death?

PROPHECIES OF COMFORT (40:1–66:24)

Since Isaiah had a lengthy ministry, chapters 40–66 were probably written later in his life. At the time of the writing, Babylon had emerged as a major power, although it would still be many years before Babylon would establish itself as the supreme power (612–539 B.C.).

Chapter 40 looks into the future, envisioning that day when Judah is in captivity in Babylon, awaiting divine deliverance.

Chapters 40–48 anticipate Cyrus, God's servant, whom the Lord used to free Israel from captivity in 538 B.C.

Chapters 49–57 view Messiah as the Servant, providing salvation and inaugurating the millennial kingdom.

Chapters 58–66 view Israel, the restored nation in the millennium, as the Lord's servant.

COMFORT OF RESTORATION (40:1–48:22)

These chapters look to the future day when Judah, in captivity in Babylon, will be divinely rescued and restored to their own land.

Introduction (40:1–11)

God brings a message of comfort to Israel in captivity; its period of discipline in Babylon is over; its sins have been paid for. It has received the disciplinary punishment for its sins (v. 2).

In preparation for God to act, the nation needed to prepare spiritually. While Isaiah called the nation to prepare spiritually for the Lord, the Gospel writers apply these words to John the

Baptist in anticipation of Christ's appearing to the nation (cp. Matt. 3:3). Using hyperbole, the prophet called the people to smooth a highway in the desert, lifting up the valleys and lowering the mountains. These words demand a spiritual renewal in preparation for Messiah's advent (vv. 3–5). Only as hearts are prepared in repentance, can Messiah's kingdom come (v. 5; Matt. 3:2; 4:17). This envisions the future day when Israel as a people will repent and Messiah's glorious kingdom will be established (Zech. 12:10–14; 14:9).

Isaiah, like other Old Testament prophets, did not distinguish between the first and second comings of Christ. This message was heralded to Israel at Christ's first coming, but only at His Second Coming will the nation repent and Messiah's kingdom be established on earth.

Amid Israel's captivity in Babylon, they would wonder how they would be released from captivity to the mighty Babylonians. God answers: People are like grass, which withers and falls (vv. 6–8). Like a hot desert wind, God would merely blow on the Babylonians and they would disappear like grass. In contrast to the temporality of humanity, God's word remains. It is forever true; it will be completely fulfilled. God's word is trustworthy. All that He has spoken will be fulfilled.

A traveler to Judah will bring the message to Jerusalem and the cities of Judah. The Israelites will be released from captivity and will return to the land (v. 9). How would it happen? "Here is your God!" declares Isaiah. He will do it! (v. 9). The Lord is pictured coming in power (v. 10).

God's arm

God's arm indicates His power (cp. 40:10; 51:5, 9; 52:10; 53:1; 59:1, 16; 60:4; 62:8; 63:5, 12).

With His strength, the Lord will rescue Israel, return them to the land, and inaugurate the millennial kingdom. Isaiah did not envision the time gap between the two comings of Christ. He merged the two comings into one, anticipating the inauguration of the messianic kingdom when Israel returned from captivity in Babylon. Like a tender shepherd carrying the weak lambs, so the Lord will bring the Israelites back into the Promised Land (v. 11).

Shepherd

The Lord is pictured as a shepherd (cp. Pss. 23:1; 80:1; John 10:11, 14; Heb. 13:20; 1 Pet. 2:25; 5:4). The shepherd provides for the sheep, and spiritually (Ps. 23:2). He protects the sheep from harm by attacking the enemy with His club and rescuing the sheep from precarious places with His staff (Ps. 23:4). The shepherd would protect the sheep with his life; the Good Shepherd dies for His sheep that they may live (John 10:11).

Sovereignty of God (40:12–41:29)

Omnipotence of God (40:12–26). God's greatness and omnipotent power are displayed in this section to remind the captive Israelites that God is greater than the Babylonians. He can free them from captivity and restore them to the land.

God's greatness is first pictured in creation (vv. 12–14). God created the oceans by scooping out the Atlantic and Pacific with each hand; He created the heavens by merely raising His outstretched hand.

A span is approximately nine inches, the distance from the little finger to the thumb when the hand is outstretched.

God has measured the dust of the earth and knows the weight of the majestic mountains (v. 12). God is peerless (v. 13). He consulted no one; He learned from no one when He created the world (v. 14). He is both omnipotent and infinitely wise. Hence, the nations—like Babylon—are like a drop of water on the edge of a pail or a speck of dust on a pair of scales—insignificant. The nations are nothing before the Lord—and less than nothing because of their moral corruption (v. 17). Babylon is less than nothing before the Lord. In His omnipotent power, the Lord will readily bring the suffering Israelites back to their land.

God is incomparable (vv. 18–20). He can only be contrasted with idols that men make with their hands, whether an expensive idol fashioned with gold and silver or a poor man's idol, made out of wood. By contrast, God sits enthroned in heaven ruling over the earth and universe (v. 22). Earth's people are merely grasshoppers in His sight; the universe is only a curtain to God that He opens. Hence, God controls the nations of the world, deposing them at will (v. 23). Earth's rulers are like a grain field: in only a short time the crop is planted; then God merely blows on it like the hot east wind and it disappears. So God will depose the Babylons and reduce them to nothing (Dan. 2:21; 4:35). God can do this; He has no equal. He is incomparable (v. 25). God knows the names of all the stars and their number and leads them out to shine in the heavens. Similarly, God will lead His people Israel home from Babylon.

Sustaining Power of God (40:27–31). Yet Israel, languishing in captivity in Babylon, thought God had forgotten them (v. 27). But they were wrong. God had a complete understanding of them; further, God never became tired that He should fail to help them (v. 28). God will bring them home from Babylon and He will give them strength for the journey. They will run and walk with physical and spiritual joy, returning to the land of their fathers (v. 31).

I visited a man in the hospital who told me, "I've been depressed for twenty-five years." Perhaps this man had forgotten the magnitude of God's greatness. When we focus on ourselves, it is easy to become depressed. But when we focus our attention and thoughts on God, we will be encouraged, recognizing that He is sovereign and omnipotent. He is greater than any problem or dilemma we face.

Writing ca. 700 B.C., Isaiah looked ahead to the day when Judah would be taken captive to Babylon. In that foreign land the Israelites would be discouraged, thinking they would never return to Judah. But God is sovereign and omnipotent; He is greater than the nations. Like a shepherd, the Lord will bring the captives home.

God's Sovereignty in History (41:1–7). Because the Lord has a unique relationship to Israel, He issued a challenge to the Gentile nations. It is a courtroom scene (v. 1). Who is like the sovereign God? It is the Lord who has raised up Cyrus the Persian from the east (v. 2; 44:28; 45:1). God goes before Cyrus, delivering the nations into his hands; God will give the Babylonian Empire into Cyrus's hands to conquer (v. 2). God is the one who accomplishes Cyrus's victories; it is God who brings forth one generation after another (v. 4). Although the nations would tremble at the advance of Cyrus, encouraging one another to withstand him, they would not be successful (vv. 5–7).

Coastlands

"Coastlands" (NASB) was the term used in the Old Testament to designate Europe. "Coastlands" together with "peoples" ("nations") designates all the people of the world.

God's Protection of Israel (41:8–20). Israel was in a special relationship to the Lord; Israel was God's "servant"; He had chosen Jacob to be the father of Israel. God chose Abraham and brought him into the Promised Land (vv. 8–9). Therefore, the people of Israel should not fear or worry (v. 10). God would bring them back into their own land. For this reason, those who assaulted Israel would fail (vv. 11–12). Instead, because the Lord was their Redeemer who upheld them (vv. 13–14), Israel would conquer their former oppressors (vv. 15–16). These last two verses anticipate the millennial kingdom when the nations of the world will be subservient to Israel (2:2–4; 19:18–25; Zech. 14:16–21). Isaiah again looks to that future day when Messiah will inaugurate the millennial kingdom. In that day the desert will blossom. There will be spiritual refreshment (vv. 17–18). God will change the topography, making seven (the number of perfection) different kinds of trees to blossom in the desert (v. 19). And the basis for God's blessing will be Israel's conversion and faith in the Messiah (v. 20).

God's Challenge to the Idols (41:21–29). God challenges the nations of the world to employ their idols to predict the future (vv. 21–23). But they will fail, and in their failure the people will realize that their pagan gods are worthless. Like the nations, they are nothing (v. 24; 40:17). But by contrast, the Lord summons Cyrus, who will trample Israel's enemies like feet trampling clay (v. 25). No one but the Lord has known or declared this; none of the idols knew this. Only Jerusalem knew in advance of Cyrus's coming. So the idols are false and worthless, mere "wind."

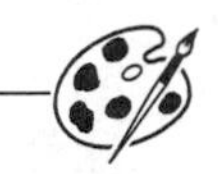

Servant

"Servant" has several meanings; the context should determine which it is. (1) It may refer to Cyrus (41:2–4; 44:28; 45:1). (2) It may refer to the nation Israel (41:8–9; 42:19; 44:1–2, 21, 26; 45:4). (3) It may refer to the remnant within the nation (43:10; 48:20; 49:3). (4) It may refer to the Messiah (42:1; 49:5–7; 50:10; 52:13; 53:11).

Servant of the Lord (42:1–25)

This chapter presents the first "servant song." The "servant" is an important theme in Isaiah. "Servant" may refer to the nation Israel, the godly remnant, or the Messiah. The context will indicate which aspect is emphasized.

Presentation of the Servant (42:1–4). Matthew 12:18–21 applies these verses to Christ. He is the One in whom the Father delights, the One on whom He has put His Spirit (Matt. 3:16; John 1:32). He will bring justice to this world (9:7; 11:3–4). Unlike the Pharisees, Messiah will not be quarrelsome (v. 2), nor will He crush the feeble; He will be gentle and kind, consoling the weak (vv. 3–4).

Servant

The "Servant" may be seen in the form of a pyramid. At the base is the nation Israel; they were meant to be God's servant, a light to the nations—but they failed. At the narrower part of the pyramid is the faithful remnant of Israel; but at the apex of the pyramid is the Messiah, who fulfills the true role of Servant. He is the Servant that God intended for the nation to be. This chapter describes Jesus Christ as the Servant.

Mission of the Servant (42:5–9). The Lord, as Creator of heaven and earth, gives power to the Servant to perform His task. The Servant will be both a covenant for the people Israel (v. 6; 49:8), and a light to the Gentiles (vv. 6, 16; 9:2; 49:6; Luke 1:79). Whereas Cyrus would release Israel from their prison in Babylon, the ultimate release from prison will be Messiah's glorious kingdom reign when people are released from the prison of sin, when their physical and spiritual eyes are opened. Idols cannot foretell this future age; only the Lord can predict Cyrus freeing the Jews in Babylon and Messiah establishing His kingdom (vv. 8–9).

Triumph of the Servant (42:10–17). Because the Lord brings light to the nations, people will praise the Lord (vv. 10–13). People who live by the sea, on the islands, in the desert—all should give glory to the Lord. God has kept silent for a long time, but now He will speak. The Servant will judge the nations ("mountains and hills") that have not acknowledged the Messiah at His Second Coming (v. 15; cp. Rev. 8:7–9:21).

Discipline of the Servant (42:18–25). These verses view the nation as the Servant. The nation had been deaf and blind, unable to hear or see God's work; they were incapable of being God's light to the nations (vv. 18–20). God had given Israel His glorious law but they repudiated it, and for that reason God disciplined the nation by taking them captive to Babylon—something He had promised to do (vv. 21–22; Deut. 28:49–53, 64–68). But even though God's anger was spent on Israel in discipline, they still failed to understand (vv. 23–25).

God had set aside His Servant, who would rescue His people Israel. The Servant in the near future is Cyrus, who will conquer the Babylonians and release the Jews from captivity in Babylon in 539 B.C. The Servant in the distant future is Messiah, who will bring back the Jews from the nations of the world and bless them in the millennial kingdom.

ASSURANCE OF RESTORATION (43:1–44:5)

Israel need not fear because the Lord is their God; He will bring them back from captivity in Babylon.

"But now"

"But now" is a feature of these chapters (43:1; 44:1; 49:5; 52:5; 64:8). Although Israel had constantly scorned and rejected the love of God, "but now" indicates God takes the initiative in blessing the nation.

Promise of Comfort to the Remnant (43:1–7). Israel stood in a unique relationship to God: Israel was the creation of God, redeemed by God, called by God (v. 1), loved by God and precious (v. 4), adopted by God (v. 6), and created for His glory (v. 7). Therefore, Israel need not fear. Although God will discipline them, He will also rescue them and restore them to the land from captivity in Babylon. But Isaiah also looked to the future, when God would discipline Israel in the tribulation ("pass through the waters . . . walk through the fire") (43:2). Yet God would be with them; He would preserve them through the tribulation and bring them back from the Gentile nations where they have been scattered (v. 6; Ezek. 36:24; 37:21; Matt. 24:31).

Purpose of God for the Remnant (43:8–13). In a courtroom scene, God summons Israel (v. 8) and the Gentiles (v. 9) to observe that He is the only true God. Who among them can proclaim

The Christian faith is absolutely unique. In the Old Testament God revealed Himself as monotheistic, as the only God, distinct from all other so-called gods (Deut. 6:4). In the New Testament, Jesus reveals Himself to be God and uniquely the Savior; there is no other Savior and no other way of salvation (John 14:6; Acts 4:12).

future events? (v. 9). None. But Israel is God's witness. The nation can testify that the Lord is God and there is no other (vv. 10–11). The Lord redeemed them from captivity in Egypt, and He will also rescue them from Babylon. By redeeming Israel, God demonstrated that He alone is God; there is no Savior apart from Him. Israelites were to be God's witnesses, testifying that He alone is the Savior.

Power of God for the Remnant (43:14–21). The Lord was the One who sent Israel to captivity in Babylon, but He would also bring them back. God promised to destroy the Babylonian power (v. 14). Just as He opened a path through the Red Sea, rescuing them from Egypt and drowning the Egyptian army (vv. 16–17), so He would rescue them again. But now God will do something new; He will make a road in the desert, a river in the desert, to bring the Israelites home (v. 19). This return from Babylon anticipated Israel's final return to the land when Messiah would establish the millennial kingdom (43:5–6).

Plea of God to the Remnant (43:22–28). Despite God's past blessings and promised future blessings, Israel failed to repent of its sins; they had become weary of God, weary of worshiping Him as He had instructed (vv. 22–24). They had, in fact, wearied God with their sinning (v. 24). Yet God would forgive their sins (v. 25), but because of Israel's history of sinning, God would first discipline them (vv. 26–28).

Provision of God for Future Blessing (44:1–5). "But now" reflects the transition from discipline to blessing. Despite Israel's disobedience, God will bring the nation into future blessing. Once more the special relationship of Israel to the Lord is evident: God chose Israel, made Israel, and formed Israel from its beginning (vv. 1–2). The Lord calls the nation "Jeshurun," meaning "the upright one," a term of endearment (Deut. 32:15; 33:5). With the advent of the millennial kingdom, the Lord will pour out His Spirit on believing Israel (Ezek. 36; 26–27; Joel 2:28) and they will prosper in the land (Ezek. 34:27; 36:28–30). God will bless Israel physically and spiritually in the millennium.

Titles of God

God is revealed by several titles: He is Lord; this is His name in His covenant relationship with Israel (v. 6; Exod. 6:2–3). He is King (v. 6); He rules sovereignly over all humanity (Ps. 2). He is Redeemer (v. 6); He rescued Israel from bondage in Egypt and He will spiritually redeem Israel (Jer. 31:31–34). He is eternal—"first" and "last" (v. 6; Rev. 1:17; 22:13). The Lord alone is God; there is no other (v. 6; Deut. 6:4).

Witness of the Restored Nation (44:6–23)

God is incomparable; there is no other like Him. He is Israel's King and Redeemer—and His people are to bear witness of His greatness and His uniqueness (v. 8). They are witnesses of God's redeeming power.

By contrast, idolatry is futile (v. 9). Idol makers themselves realize that idols cannot see or know; they are witnesses of the futility of idols. Those who make idols are only men, not God, and they will be in terror of the only and true God (v. 11). The idol maker (blacksmith, v. 12; carpenter, v. 13) carefully fashions the idols with his tools so that it consumes all his energy (vv. 12–13), and he goes to great lengths in procuring choice woods for his idols (v. 14). But some of the wood he uses to build a fire and cook a meal while he uses the other wood to fashion an idol which he worships (vv. 15–17)! These idols cannot see or think—they are ignorant (v. 18). The idol maker is foolish, worshiping a piece of wood that is nothing more than a pile of ashes (v. 20). He is deceived. The idol cannot help him.

Verses 21–23 carry forward the theme of joy of verses 6–8. In contrast to the futility of idolatry, the Lord has redeemed Israel, wiping out its sins. The nation has been disciplined in Babylon; now the Lord, their Redeemer, will bring

We probably don't think we are capable of worshiping idols. But is it possible? Can there be idols in my life that I am worshiping? What does John mean when he says, "Guard yourselves from idols"? (1 John 5:21, NASB).

them back to the land. For this reason the nation can shout for joy.

- *God is unique. He alone is sovereign and omnipotent; He is Israel's Redeemer. By contrast, idols are nothing. They neither see, think, nor act. They are futile, and idol makers are foolish. Israel bears witness to God's greatness and His redeeming power.*

Fulfillment of Restoration (44:24–45:25)

Prediction of Cyrus (44:24–28). God reminded Israel that He is the Lord of creation (v. 24) and He is also Lord of history. He will raise up Cyrus the Persian to allow the Jews to return to the land and rebuild the city of Jerusalem (vv. 26, 28; Ezra 1).

Josephus, the Jewish historian of Jesus' day, comments on the fact that Cyrus is mentioned by name: "This was known to Cyrus by his reading the book which Isaiah left behind him of his prophecies. . . . Accordingly, when Cyrus read this, and admired the divine power, an earnest desire and ambition seized upon him to fulfil what was so written; so he called for the most eminent Jews that were in Babylon, and said to them, that he gave them leave to go back to their own country, and to rebuild their city Jerusalem, and the temple of God" *(Antiquities of the Jews, XI.1.)*

Restoration Through Cyrus (45:1–8). Because the Lord had anointed Cyrus, the Lord would prepare the way for the Persian king to conquer Babylon (45:1–2). God would give Cyrus the wealth of the conquered nations (v. 3). But God would bless Cyrus because of Israel, His servant and chosen people (v. 4). For that reason alone Cyrus would be given a special name and title of honor. The sovereign God, who alone is uniquely God, will bring it to pass. He will empower Cyrus so that all people will recognize the Lord, who brings blessing and calamity alike, has done this (vv. 6–7). God's blessing of Israel anticipates the future blessing in the millennium (v. 8).

Vindication of the Lord (45:9–13). God is sovereign; people in the world have no more right to question the ways of God than a clay pot can question the work of the potter (v. 9) or a child can question why his parents brought him into existence (v. 10). The Lord is the sovereign One who created the earth and the heavens, and He will also raise up Cyrus to set Israel free and rebuild Jerusalem (v. 13).

Nebuchadnezzar, king of Babylon, destroyed and burned Jerusalem in 586 B.C., and took the Hebrew people captive to Babylon (2 Kings 25:1–12). But in 539 B.C. Cyrus of the Medo-Persian Empire conquered Babylon and issued a decree permitting the Jews to return to Jerusalem and rebuild the city—and Cyrus financed the project (Ezra 6:4)!

Humiliation of the Nations (45:14–17). Isaiah again looked to the distant future: In the millennium the Gentile nations would be subject to Israel; they would bring their wealth to Israel (Zech. 14:14, 19). In that day they will acknowledge the Lord as the true God (v. 14). Though during Israel's captivity in Babylon it seemed God was hiding Himself (v. 15), the idolatrous pagan nations will be humiliated when the Lord rescues Israel out of the tribulation (v. 17; 43:2). Israel will never again be ashamed of their Redeemer (Rom. 11:26; 1 Pet. 2:6).

Invitation to the Nations (45:18–25). The sovereign, omnipotent Lord did not create the world to be empty. The land of Israel, emptied during the Babylonian captivity, would soon be populated (v. 18). God spoke the truth openly—and it would come to pass (v. 19). The Lord invites the Gentile nations to be saved (v. 20); as the sovereign God, He alone has declared the future. The Lord alone is able to save the Gentiles (v. 22)—and some will be saved (v. 24a), but some will reject Him (v. 24b). Nonetheless, in that future day when Jesus Christ establishes His millennial reign, every knee will bow to His authority (v. 23; Phil. 2:10–11).

Cyrus is called "Shepherd" (44:28) and "Anointed" ("Messiah") (45:1). He is the only human king ever called "Anointed" or "Messiah." Cyrus was "anointed" by God to shepherd God's people Israel by permitting them to return to their land. Cyrus prefigures Jesus Christ, the Messiah at the end of the age who will regather believing Israel and return them to the land (Matt. 24:31).

The Lord's words in Isaiah ring out: The Lord alone is God; there is none else. Some theologians are proposing that people who have never heard of Christ may nonetheless be saved. But that is not biblical teaching. "Turn to me and be saved . . . for I am God, and there is no other" (v. 22) is an exclusive statement. There is no allowance for other gods or other ways of salvation.

- *The Lord will raise up Cyrus the Persian to conquer the Babylonians and set free the captive Israelites, enabling them to return to their land. Cyrus, the Lord's anointed, prefigures Jesus Christ, the Lord's Anointed, who will establish the millennial kingdom and restore Israel to its land. In that day all Gentile nations will submit to the Lord's authority.*

Preservation and Restoration from Babylon (46:1–47:15)

Since the Lord has raised up Cyrus to deliver Israel from Babylon, these chapters detail Babylon's collapse, along with its gods.

Bel

Bel is the Babylonian form of the Canaanite god, Baal, the god of storm and agriculture. His name is found in the name Belshazzar. Nebo was Bel's son, the god of learning, and is found in the name Nebuchadnezzar. The pagan idols were transported in public processions.

Insignificance of the Babylonian Gods (46:1–7). The Babylonian gods that ought to have helped them had become a hindrance to the Babylonians as the animals struggled in carting the idols with them on festivals (vv. 1–2). These gods could not help them, but by contrast the Lord carried Israel from their beginnings to their old age (vv. 3–4). The repetition "I shall bear you . . . I shall carry you . . . I shall bear you . . . I shall deliver you" is a strong reminder of God's faithfulness in rescuing Israel from Babylon and bringing them safely into the land (v. 4, NASB). Israel's omnipotent God is incomparable. Certainly He cannot be compared with the pagan idols that are made out of silver and gold. These idols are carried from place to place. Yet they themselves cannot move or help anyone (vv. 6–7)

Sovereign Control of God (46:8–13). As the sovereign, unique God, the Lord decrees and declares all things—the end from the beginning (v. 10). He controls the future; He has planned Israel's restoration and He will accomplish it (v. 10). He will do it through Cyrus, who comes from the east like a bird of prey against the Babylonians (v. 11). The stubborn and unrighteous Babylonians would be defeated by "my righteousness"—Cyrus (v. 13). That would result in salvation for Israel—their rescue from Babylon (v. 13).

We often make the mistake of carrying our anxieties and burdens when the Lord will carry them for us. He will carry them from our birth to our old age—forever! (see 1 Pet. 5:7).

Song of Triumph over Babylon (47:1–15). In a song of triumph, this chapter describes Babylon's fall from power and conquest by the Persians in 539 B.C. Defeated Babylon is pictured sitting in the dust in humiliation and disgrace (v. 1). The nation is seen as a slave, turning the large millstone in grinding grain (v. 2). Babylon will be reduced to a half-naked slave girl toiling as a slave (vv. 2–3). This would be a new experience for Babylon, the "virgin daughter," so called because she had never been destroyed (v. 1). But Babylon would be deposed and no longer be the queen of kingdoms (v. 5). God had been angry with Israel and disciplined them by sending them to Babylon, but the Babylonians showed them no mercy (v. 6). Babylon failed to think of the consequences (v. 7).

In 539 B.C., Belshazzar held a great drinking feast for one thousand nobles (Dan. 5:1). He desecrated the vessels from Solomon's Temple by using them in his drunken state as he drank in praise of his pagan gods (Dan. 5:4). He felt secure in Babylon, a walled city, 14 miles square, surrounded by a moat and with outer walls 87 feet thick and 350 feet high.

In her pride Babylon thought she would never be defeated; this impenetrable city was secure (v. 8). Not so. Pictured as a wife and mother, Babylon would suddenly become a widow and childless (v. 9). Its witchcraft and demonic forces would not help them (v. 9). Babylon's pride was its downfall; it proclaimed the prerogatives of deity for itself (v. 10)—prerogatives that belong to God alone (43:11; 44:6; 45:5–6). But now disaster and destruction would suddenly come upon this pagan nation (Dan. 5).

The Lord taunts Babylon, inviting its astrologers to help the people (vv. 12–15; Dan. 2:2, 10). But their gods would fail; Babylon would be destroyed, burned up like stubble (v. 14).

The Babylonian gods were inept, incapable of rescuing Babylon from the coming disaster. God called Cyrus the Persian from the east to conquer Babylon and release the Israelites to return to their homeland.

Admonition to the Restored Nation (48:1–22)

Concerning Obstinacy (48:1–11). Speaking to the nation that in the future would be captive in Babylon, the Lord indicted them for their hypocrisy and obstinacy. They swore by the Lord's name and called themselves citizens of Jerusalem, yet they were comfortable in Babylon, unwilling to return to Jerusalem. They were stubborn; they were idolatrous. For that reason God told them ahead of time what He would do—something the idols could not do (vv. 3, 5).

We probably never think in terms of idols; yet we create idols when we trust in something other than the Lord. Perhaps we place our security in our stable financial condition, our job, our education, our social standing—but these will fail us. Our trust and confidence must be in the Lord alone.

Israel had ignored God's previous prophecies; now the Lord would tell them new things—things they had not heard before (vv. 6–8). God had disciplined them, refined them in the fire of affliction in Babylon (v. 10); now He would bring them back into the Promised Land, in spite of their rebellion (v. 8). God was acting in concert with His name in bringing them back to the land (vv. 9, 11). He is a God of mercy and grace who will preserve His people.

Concerning Observing God's Greatness (48:12–16). The Lord again reminded the negligent nation of His great power. He is the One who created the earth and the vast heavens, calling them into being (v. 13). Because of His great power, the Lord will judge Babylon—something the idols could not do (v. 14). The Lord will summon Cyrus of Persia, giving him success in destroying the Babylonians (v. 15). The Lord has not kept this a secret (v. 16). Verse 16b is a trinitarian statement: "the Lord God . . . Me . . . His Spirit" (NASB). Just as Cyrus will accomplish God's will, so the Messiah, whom the Father has sent and upon whom He has placed His Spirit (Matt. 12:18), will triumph over the nations and inaugurate the messianic kingdom.

"Chaldeans" is a synonym for Neo-Babylon. Chaldeans represents the tribes, along with Sumerians and Akkadians, that lived in southeast Mesopotamia. The original Babylonian Empire was conquered by the Assyrians. Later, Nabopolassar led the Neo-Babylonians (Chaldeans) to a victory over the Assyrians by destroying Nineveh in 612 B.C. Under Nebuchadnezzar the Chaldean (Neo-Babylonian) Empire reached its zenith.

Concerning Obedience (48:17–22). The principle of Deuteronomy 28 is evident here: Obedience brings blessing, while disobedience brings chastisement. If only Israel had obeyed the Lord, the nation would have entered into innumerable blessings; their progeny would have mushroomed instead of dying in captivity in a foreign land (Gen. 22:17; vv. 18–19). Just as the Israelites fled Egypt when the Lord redeemed them, so they are commanded to flee Babylon, amid joyful singing of the Lord's redemption (v. 20). And as the Lord provided for Israel in the wilderness as they fled Egypt (Exod. 17:1–7; Num. 20:11), so the Lord will provide for the Israelites as they return from Babylon (35:6; 43:19–20). But for the wicked among them, there will be no peace (v. 22).

Like the Israelites, it is easy to get into a routine of church attendance, giving, singing, worshiping—but all without heart. Inside there may be stubborn resistance to God's Word and will. God may take us into the "divine woodshed" to discipline us to get our attention so we will take His Word seriously.

Because of Israel's stubbornness and obstinacy, the Lord disciplined them by sending them into captivity in Babylon. But now He promised to bring them back, calling Cyrus to do His bidding—something the pagan idols could not do.

QUESTIONS TO GUIDE YOUR STUDY

1. To whom was Isaiah's prophecy of comfort directed (chaps. 40–66)?
2. What are the various meanings of *servant*?
3. What did the Jewish historian Josephus tell us about Cyrus?
4. What did God anoint Cyrus to do?
5. With what earlier event in Israel's history did Isaiah compare the return from Babylon to Judah?

COMFORT OF REDEMPTION (49:1–55:13)

These chapters deal with Israel's redemption, accomplished by the Servant (Messiah). He will both atone for their sins and restore them to the land in the millennial kingdom.

Mission of the Servant (49:1–26)

His Designation (49:1–4). The Servant calls to the Gentile nations, to whom He will also bring salvation. God called Him from conception (cp. Luke 1:31–33) for a specific ministry. He is destined to rule over the nations; from His mouth comes a sharp sword, His Word, which will subdue the nations (v. 2; Rev. 19:15). Messiah is the true Servant, Israel; He is all that God intended Israel to be—a light bringing salvation to the Gentiles (v. 3). Despite little evidence of Israel's response, the Servant trusts in the Lord to accomplish Israel's redemption.

His Commission (49:5–6). The Servant's commission, which was established before His birth, is to restore Israel in a spiritual relationship to God (Ezek. 36:25–27) and in a physical relationship to the land (Luke 1:33). But the Servant's ministry will also include the Gentiles; the

Servant will bring spiritual light to the nations of the world (v. 6; 9:1–2; 42:6; Luke 1:79).

His Rejection (49:7). The Servant will initially be rejected by those He came to save. He will be the despised One (53:3), rejected (50:6–7; 52:13–53:12; Matt. 12:24; 27:22–25). But one day kings and princes will bow down to the Servant (Phil. 2:10; Rev. 19:15–19).

His Blessings (49:8–13). In redeeming Israel the Servant will fulfill the covenant with His people—He will restore them to the land (v. 8). He will gather them from the nations of the world, protecting and providing for them as He brings them home to the land (vv. 9–11). From the north and west they will come back to the land as the Servant-Messiah brings them into millennial blessings. All of nature is pictured responding with joy as Israel is restored to the land (v. 13).

His Reassurance (49:14–26). Although Israel thought the Lord had forsaken them (v. 14; 40:27), the Lord could no more forget Israel than a mother could forget her child (v. 15). Jerusalem was engraved on the Lord's hands, so to speak; the Lord remembers the walls of Jerusalem (v. 16). Those who have destroyed Jerusalem will leave; those who rebuild Jerusalem will return (v. 17). The city that previously was desolate will be thronged with people and with their own children; like ornaments they will crowd the city (vv. 18–20). They will be astonished at their innumerable descendants (v. 21).

"Jews had a custom of marking on their hands, or elsewhere, a delineation of the city and the temple, as a sign of their devotion to, and perpetual remembrance of, them" (W. E. Vine, *Isaiah*, p. 147).

In verse 22 Isaiah looks to the distant future, when Israelites will be restored to the land from the Gentile nations. Gentiles will assist them in their safe return; kings will be subservient to Israel, acknowledging the supremacy of

Messiah in the millennium (v. 23; Matt. 25:31–32; Phil. 2:10). But those nations that have oppressed Israel will be judged (vv. 24–26; Joel 3:1–3; Matt. 25:31–46). The Lord will rescue His people from the nations (v. 24; Matt. 24:31) and punish the nations that persecuted Israel (vv. 25–26). The Lord is Israel's Savior and Redeemer.

Submission of the Servant (50:1–11)

The nation Israel is contrasted with the Servant, the Messiah: the nation is disobedient; the Servant is obedient and submissive to God's will.

Disobedience of Israel (50:1–3). Like a man who gave his wife a divorce certificate and sent her away (Deut. 24:1), so the Lord sent Israel away into captivity because of its sins. Israel's captivity was not because the Lord was unable to protect the nation; He is omnipotent (v. 3). The nation was sent into captivity as a slave because of sin.

Obedience of the Servant (50:4–9). In contrast to Israel's disobedience (vv. 1–3), the Servant (Messiah) is obedient. Even when He was rejected by His people, scourged, and spit on, He was an obedient, submissive Servant (v. 6; John 19:1; Matt. 26:67; 27:30). He purposed to fulfill His mission (v. 7), and God would vindicate Him (vv. 8–9).

Exhortation of the Servant (50:10–11). In this epilogue the prophet exhorted the people who were walking in darkness to fear the Servant. Those who trust in the Lord and obey the Servant will receive comfort, but those who "light fires," who devise their own way, will face punishment.

The Lord called the Servant (the Messiah) to restore Israel spiritually and physically to the Promised Land. Israel was not forgotten; He would bring the nation back from captivity. Although He was rejected, He would fulfill God's purpose and ultimately bring blessing to Israel as well as Gentile nations in the millennium.

Christ is our example in suffering while submitting to the will of God. When He was reviled, He did not retaliate but kept entrusting Himself to the Father (1 Pet. 2:23). We are called to "follow in his steps" (1 Pet. 2:21).

Provision by the Servant (51:1–52:12)

Reminder of God's Past Help (51:1–3). The Lord encouraged the godly remnant ("you who pursue righteousness") within Israel to look to Abraham, their father and founder; the rock from which they were cut. God blessed Abraham (Gen. 17:1–8; 22:17) and He would bless Zion—Jerusalem in the millennium when the land of Israel becomes like Eden.

Reassurance of Israel's Future (51:4–8). In the millennial kingdom God's word and justice will govern all the nations (v. 4). That day when the Lord will rule in the millennium is approaching; in that day the present heavens and earth will be renovated (65:17; 2 Pet. 3:10) but the Lord's salvation and His righteousness will remain forever (v. 6; 9:7). Knowing God has established their future, the believing remnant should not fear the insults of men (v. 7). Like those who oppose the Servant (50:8), those who oppose them will be eaten by moths (v. 8).

Rahab is a mythical sea monster that represents Egypt. Rahab being "cut to pieces" and "pierced" represents the armies of Egypt being destroyed in the Red Sea (Exod. 14:26–31).

Reassurance of God's Protection (51:9–16). Verses 9–11 record either the prophet's words or the prayer of the righteous remnant for God to act in the future as He has in the past. Just as the Lord rescued Israel from bondage in Egypt, so the call is for God to act on behalf of the Israelites in bondage in Babylon. God will act! The Israelites will return from Babylon amid joyful singing (v. 11).

The Lord responded in verses 12–16, reminding the nation of His greatness. Because the Lord, Creator of heaven and earth, is the One who comforts them, they should not fear the Babylonians (vv. 12–13). They are simply grass that will burn up; they will be destroyed by the Medo-Persians. The Israelites will not die in Babylon; their captivity will soon be over (v. 14). The Lord will raise up Cyrus the Persian, who will come against the Babylonians like a roaring wave (v. 15). God will protect His people (v. 16)!

When we forget the Lord's greatness and when we look at circumstances, we are afraid. That is foolish and wrong. Isn't God greater than any calamity we encounter? Hasn't He who created the universe all power to act on our behalf? Furthermore, worry doesn't help! Jesus instructed us concerning worry (Matt. 6:25–34).

Reassurance of God's Forgiveness (51:17–23). The Lord calls Jerusalem: "Rouse yourself!" because God is about to bless the city. The repetitious "Rouse yourself! Rouse yourself!" (v. 17, NASB) suggests urgency. Like a drunkard inebriated by alcohol, so in the past the people of Jerusalem had drunk the cup of God's wrath—His judgment upon the sinful city. The horror of the captivity resulted—famine, destruction, death (v. 19). The people lay helpless in the streets of Jerusalem—with no one to help them. God was disciplining the sinful nation (v. 20).

But now their time of discipline is over! God will never again make them drink the cup of His wrath (v. 22). In that future millennial day the Lord will give Israel victory over their persecutors; but those nations that afflicted Israel will be judged by the Lord—they will drink the cup of God's wrath (Joel 3:1–3; Zech. 14:1–4; Matt. 25:31–46; Rev. 6:15–17).

Reassurance of Israel's Future Restoration (52:1–12). The double "awake, awake" once more arouses the Hebrew people. Jerusalem has a glorious future! Not only will the people be liberated from captivity and oppression from Gentile nations, but Jerusalem will be exalted when Messiah rules as King in the supreme city (Matt. 25:31–32). Jerusalem will no longer sit mourning in the dust; the people will no longer be taken away in chains to foreign invaders (v. 2). Although Israel was sold as slaves (50:1), the Lord has redeemed His people at no cost to them (v. 3)! In their past, they had been captives in Egypt and Assyria (v. 4) as well as in Babylon—a nation that blasphemed the Lord (v. 5). Now the Lord would set them free and in their repentant state they would know the Lord (v. 6; Ezek. 36:24–28).

Jacob's family went down to Egypt as a family in 1876 B.C. and grew to a nation that was held as slaves until the Lord freed them in 1446 B.C. (Exod. 1:5–14). In 722 B.C. the Assyrians took the ten northern tribes captive to Assyria (2 Kings 17:1–6) and in 586 B.C. the Babylonians took the remaining two tribes (the Southern Kingdom of Judah) captive to Babylon (2 Kings 25:1–12).

In the future day when Messiah returns to reign in Jerusalem (v. 7), He will bring the good news of salvation (cp. Rom. 10:15). The salvation Christ brings will result in peace because the Hebrew people will be converted (9:6–7; 26:3, 12; 54:10; 66:12). That will be a time of both spiritual and physical blessing in Jerusalem: the people will be converted and the city will be restored to its preeminent place among the nations (v. 9). All the nations will recognize the supremacy of the Messiah and the city of Jerusalem (v. 10). In verses 11 and 12 the prophet returns to the historical context, instructing the people to separate themselves from the Gentiles and return to the land of Israel. Apparently some wanted the security of remaining in that pagan nation.

Believers have a glorious future. Sometimes we get so entangled with the affairs of life that we forget the magnificent future God is preparing for us (John 14:2–3). The realization of our sublime future should fill us with peace and joy (Rev. 21:1–4).

- *The nation Israel is exhorted to look in faith*
- *to the future. The Lord, who is omnipotent,*
- *will rescue Israel from the nations, bring*
- *them back into the land, and bless them in*
- *Messiah's rule in the millennial kingdom. No*
- *longer will the Gentile nations afflict them.*

Substitution of the Servant (52:13–53:12)

This section strikes at the heart of the Servant passage. It depicts the Servant in His suffering, providing the basis by which the Lord will bless Israel. It is only through atonement for sin that God can bless Israel. The Servant, Jesus Christ, provides that atonement through His substitutionary death on behalf of Israel and all people.

Exaltation of the Servant (52:13–15). The ascending phrases "high and lifted up, and greatly exalted" (v. 13, NASB) indicate the Servant will be lifted up to the height of God Himself (the same term is used in 6:1). Some suggest this refers to Christ's resurrection, ascension, and exaltation to the right hand of the Father. It ultimately focused on His exaltation (Acts 2:31–33; 3:13; Phil. 2:9–11; Col. 3:1; Heb. 1:3; 8:1; 10:12; 12:2; 1 Pet. 3:22).

Sprinkle

"Sprinkle" identifies the O.T. custom when the priest dipped his finger in blood and sprinkled the blood before the veil of the sanctuary and also sprinkled some blood on the horns of the altar (Lev. 4:6, 7, 18, 25, 30, 35). It symbolized cleansing from sin.

Prior to the Servant's exaltation is His humiliation (v. 14). When the Servant was scourged, people looked away in horror because of His marred appearance—He was hardly recognizable (v. 14; John 19:1). But through His crucifixion the Servant sprinkle many nations, i.e., cleanse them from sin (v. 15). Even kings will be speechless when they recognize the magnitude of the Servant's atonement on their behalf (v. 15).

Humiliation of the Servant (53:1–12). *His rejection by men* (53:1–3). Although the message about the Servant is sublime, few would respond to the message (v. 1). The people failed to recognize His greatness; they only saw Him in His humble ancestry, one who came from the Davidic line ("tender shoot"; cp. 11:1) and from a spiritually deprived area ("dry ground"). He did not have the attractiveness of royalty (v. 2); in fact, He was despised and rejected by people (v. 3). He was not held in esteem; the people failed to see His importance (John 1:10–11). People found Him repulsive and avoided contact with Him (v. 3).

His atoning for men (53:4–6). The Servant suffered a substitutionary, atoning death on behalf of people (vv. 4–6). When Christ healed the sick in His earthly ministry, He fulfilled Isaiah 53:4 (Matt. 8:16–17). In His life Christ fulfilled the prophecy related to people's sicknesses; in His death Christ fulfilled the prophecy related to people's sins. Christ's atoning death paid the penalty for sin, not sickness. Christ the Servant died because of our "transgressions" and "iniquities"—and through His atoning death we are spiritually healed (v. 5). Peter interpreted Christ's death as healing people from sin, not from sicknesses (1 Pet. 2:24). The need was great: "all" had gone astray; all humanity is depraved and fallen (Rom. 3:10–23; 5:12). The Lord caused the Servant to atone for the sins of the human race (Matt. 27:46; 2 Cor. 5:15, 19; Gal. 3:13; 1 Tim. 2:6; 4:10; 1 John 2:2; 4:10).

Physical healing is not in the atonement. People cannot claim health through the death of Christ. Although some people teach this, the fact is that all people ultimately get sick and die—even those who teach healing in the atonement.

The doctrine of the substitutionary atonement of Christ is crucial to our belief. Jesus did not die as a martyr or as a supreme act of love; He died as a substitute for our sins. The substitutionary nature is emphasized in the pronouns: "our . . . He . . . our . . . He . . . we . . . Him (v. 4) . . . He . . . our . . . He . . . our . . . our . . . Him . . . His . . . we" (v. 5) . . . us . . . Him" (v. 6). The substitutionary atonement of Christ is clearly taught in Scripture (Matt. 20:28; 2 Cor. 5:15; 1 Tim. 2:6; 1 Pet. 2:24).

His suffering for men (53:7–9). The Servant's atoning death was voluntary. He presented Himself to His executioners like a willing sacrificial lamb (v. 7; John 1:29; 10:18; Heb. 10:7). He was arrested and sentenced to death by the Sanhedrin and Pilate (v. 8; Matt. 26:66; 27:66). And so the Servant died for the sins of the guilty people (v. 8). In death the Servant hung between two thieves (v. 9; Matt. 27:38), yet His grave was provided by a rich man, Joseph of Arimathea (v. 9; Matt. 27:57–60). But He was innocent, sinless (v. 9; John 8:46; 1 John 3:5).

His justification of men (53:10–12). God the Father planned the Servant's death since His death was a guilt offering that atoned for the sins of the human race (v. 10). As a result, the Servant will see His offspring—He will be resurrected (v. 10; John 20:16, 19–29). But the Servant's death will result in many being justified (v. 11; Rom. 5:12–21). Like a victorious general who has conquered the enemy, the Servant will be victorious through His death, dividing the spoils of war by conquering sin and Satan (v. 12; Gen. 3:15; Matt. 12:29; Rom. 8:2–3; Heb. 2:14).

The death Christ died was for me. He died as a substitute for me. Christ did not die as a martyr, an example of bravery, or as a demonstration of love. He died as my substitute because I am guilty.
When He died, I should have died. But Christ has freed me from sin's penalty and power (Rom. 8:1–4). But I must trust in His atoning death for me. He died in my place.

- *The Servant, Jesus Christ, though rejected in life, died a substitutionary death for all mankind, atoning for the sins of the human race. As a result, Christ has conquered sin and been exalted to the right hand of the Father.*

Blessings of the Servant (54:1–55:13)

Because of the Servant's atoning death and Israel's future acceptance of the Servant's atonement, great blessing will come upon Israel.

Blessing of the Restored Nation (54:1–10). Israel is pictured as a childless mother who now will have numerous children (v. 1). Many Jews will repent and trust in the Messiah (Zech. 12:10–14; Rom. 11:25–26), so that Israel, like a tent, will need to enlarge its borders to host all the people who will live there (vv. 2–3). In fact, the Jews will be so numerous that they will spread to the nations and inhabit its previously abandoned cities (v. 3).

In Israel it was a shame and a calamity to be childless (Gen. 15:2; 29:31; 1 Sam. 1:2). But an abundance of children was evidence of the Lord's blessing (Gen. 15:5; 17:5–6; 28:14).

In that future day Israel will no longer be humiliated through its own sin or foreign oppression. The past will be forgotten (v. 4). Israel will be restored to the Lord as a wife is restored to her husband (vv. 5–6; Hos. 2:16). Although the Lord forsook Israel because of its sin, now that the nation trusts in Him, the Lord receives back His wayward wife (vv. 7–8).

Following the Flood, God promised Noah He would never again inundate the earth with a flood; similarly, the Lord promised Israel He will never again be angry with it (v. 9). Israel will never again suffer the disciplinary rod from the Lord. He will extend His loyal love and compassion to Israel so it will enjoy peace forever (v. 10; 2:2; 9:6, 7; 11:1–13).

Beauty of the Restored Nation (54:11–17). Jerusalem has been a battered city, destroyed by foreign nations, but now, in the millennial kingdom, the Lord will restore the city and rebuild the New Jerusalem on a foundation of sapphires with towers of rubies and walls of precious stones (vv. 11–12; cp. Rev. 21:10–27). The Israelites will live in the land in faith, gladly receiving the Lord's instruction (v. 13). Because they have appropriated the Messiah's righteousness, no terror will befall them (v. 14). If anyone attempts to harm Israel in that day, they will be destroyed (v. 15). In the past the Lord allowed other nations to afflict Israel, but now Israel's enemies will not survive if they assault the Lord's people (vv. 16–17). Israel is the heritage of the Lord, and because they have trusted in the Messiah, the Lord will bring them into a place of blessing.

Blessings of the Nations (55:1–13). Millennial blessings expand beyond Israel to include Gentile nations as well. The invitation is extended to include "every one," all who are spiritually thirsty. They may receive Messiah's salvation without cost since it is by grace through faith (Eph. 2:8–9). In the millennial kingdom they will enjoy the Lord's abundance, spiritually and physically (25:6; Joel 2:21–27; 3:18). Those who come to the Messiah will enjoy the everlasting benefits of the Davidic Covenant (2 Sam. 7:12–16). That covenant promised that Messiah would rule on the Davidic throne in an everlasting kingdom (cp. Luke 1:31–33). That will be fulfilled at Christ's Second Coming (Matt. 25:31). In the millennium, Messiah will be a witness to the Gentiles; He will be their leader and commander (v. 4). Then the nations will be subservient to the Messiah (v. 5; 2:3; 19:18–25; Mic. 4:1–5; Zech. 14:16–21).

Those who come to Him will receive salvation and compassion (vv. 6–7; cp. Jer. 29:13–14). The people will not be able to fathom this limitless grace and compassion from the Lord. It is because the Lord's thoughts and ways are beyond human comprehension (vv. 8–9). But God's word is powerful—just like the rain from heaven causes vegetation to grow, so God's word accomplishes precisely what He determines (v. 11). In the figure of personification, the mountains and hills are heard shouting and the trees are seen clapping their hands. All nature rejoices at the institution of the millennial kingdom with Messiah's blessing on the Hebrew people (vv. 12–13). Joy and peace will predominate in Messiah's kingdom. There will be a reversal of the effects of Adam's fall (Gen. 3:17–18); nature will be restored to Edenic conditions (Amos 9:14).

Through the provision of the Messiah's substitutionary atonement, great blessing will come to the nation Israel as they believe in the Messiah. So many Israelites will believe in the Messiah that the nation will expand its borders; Gentiles will also believe in Messiah. God's Word has promised these things, and they will be accomplished.

God's Word has promised great blessings for the future. It is imperative that we trust His word. We are called to live by faith; God has spoken—He will perform it. He has given us Christ and we enter God's blessings by believing in Christ for salvation, and we continue to believe His promises for daily blessings.

COMFORT OF MILLENNIAL JOY (56:1–66:24)

The book of Isaiah moves to its climax in these chapters, detailing Messiah's establishment of the millennial kingdom, bringing comfort to Israel and also to the Gentiles.

Inclusion of the Gentiles (56:1–8)

Chapter 55 mentioned Gentiles in general; chapter 56 lists specific groups of Gentiles that will enter into worship and fellowship with Israelites. This ultimately anticipates the millennium.

Admonition to Israel (56:1–2). In the light of the coming deliverance from Babylon, the Lord exhorts the people to righteous living. In the Old Testament era, a person was saved by grace through faith (Hab. 2:4), but the believer expressed his righteousness by living according to the Mosaic Law by which Israel was bound to the Lord (Exod. 19:1–8). A particular expression of righteousness under the Law was keeping the Sabbath (v. 2; Exod. 20:8–11).

A eunuch (lit., "bed keeper," one who has charge of beds or bed chambers), usually meant a man who had been castrated. Although Jews did not practice castration (Lev. 22:24; Deut. 23:1), other cultures like the Assyrians performed castration on their subjugated enemies. Castration was practiced in Egypt (cp. Gen. 37:36; 39:1). Eunuchs usually served in the military or over women and children (2 Kings 8:6; 9:32; 18:17; 23:11; 25:19; Acts 8:27).

Extension of Blessing (56:3–8). Under the Mosaic Law, foreigners and eunuchs were prohibited from worshiping with the Israelites (Deut. 23:1–3), but in the millennial kingdom, these will also enter into blessing. Eunuchs who keep the Sabbath and the Mosaic Law will join Israelites in worship (vv. 4–5). Even though they do not have children, God will give them a memorial and a name. Similarly, foreigners who keep the Sabbath and the Mosaic Law by offering the appropriate sacrifices will be welcomed to worship in the Temple in Jerusalem (vv. 6–7).

Condemnation of the Wicked (56:9–57:21)

This section begins a new theme, explaining the reason for Israel's captivity in Babylon.

Condemnation of Israel's Wicked Rulers (56:9–57:2). Ultimate responsibility for Israel's moral failure and depravity belonged to the nation's spiritual leaders. Hence, the Lord calls on "beasts," the Gentile powers, to devour the sinful nation (v. 9). These false religious leaders were blind watchmen. They failed to see the idolatry and spiritual depravity and sound the alarm (v. 10). They were like silent watchdogs who refused to bark when they saw the spiritual intruders destroying the spiritual house. They were dreamers who loved to sleep, failing to alert the nation about their spiritual disaster. They were greedy dogs and false shepherds, religious profiteers who were more intent on self-indulgence than on serving the Lord

(vv. 11–12; cp. Ezek. 13:1–23; 34:1–10). In that perverse environment, the righteous men were persecuted; only in death did the righteous find peace (57:1–2; cp. 2 Kings 22:20).

There is a great responsibility for all those in ministry, whether pastor or Bible class teacher, to be faithful in teaching the truth despite opposition. There is frequently the pressure to water down or tone down the message to make it more palatable to the hearers, but we must resist this temptation. We are called to faithfully teach God's Word, whether it is popular or not.

Condemnation of Idolators (57:3–13). The prophet indicted the idolaters, the apostate people in Israel, who borrowed from the pagan cultures around them. Some practiced sorcery, magic, and the casting of spells (cp. Lev. 19:26; Deut. 18:10, 14; 2 Kings 21:6; Mic. 5:12); some practiced prostitution, likely the worship of Baal and Asherah which involved temple prostitution (v. 3). And in their sinful behavior they ridiculed the righteous (v. 4).

They worshiped these gods and poured out drink offerings to them. It was on these hillsides that they committed sexual immorality in their worship of Baal and Asherah—and they committed spiritual adultery since Israel was the wife of the Lord (vv. 7–8; Hos. 1:2; 2:2). And yet Israel relentlessly searched for more pagan gods to worship (vv. 9–10).

The "oaks" and "tree" represents the pagan worship sites on the hills. The female fertility goddess Asherah, the consort of Baal, was represented by a wooden pole or tree. This pagan worship involved sexual immorality (see "Word Picture" under 27:7–13). In the ravines they offered their children as burnt offerings to the pagan god Molech (v. 5; 2 Kings 23:10; Jer. 32:35). The stone was a *massebah*, a symbol of a male deity; this worship also involved degrading sexual immorality (v. 6).

Amid the idolatry, Israel forgot the Lord—and since He was silent, they failed to fear Him (v. 11). But now the Lord would judge them. When they would cry out in fear, He would not listen to them; they could rely on their idols (vv. 11–12)! These idolaters were to be carried away in judgment, but the righteous would inherit the Promised Land (v. 13; Deut. 16:20; 30:1–10). This would ultimately be fulfilled in the millennium.

Compassion on the Repentant (57:14–21). Amid a land filled with idolatry, the Lord encouraged the godly remnant. They were encouraged to prepare for the return from Babylon (v. 14; 40:3–4). Although the Lord hid His face from them when He disciplined them in the Babylonian captivity, now the time of testing is over and the Lord comes to fellowship with the repentant Israelites (vv. 15–16; Ps. 34:18; 51:17). He will restore them to the land and comfort them. But these promises are only for the repentant. The wicked will not benefit; they will not enjoy God's peace.

Verse 15 teaches both the transcendence of God and the immanence of God. Transcendence means that God is exalted above His creatures and distinct from them (Exod. 15:11). Immanence teaches that God also condescends to fellowship with those who are "contrite and lowly of spirit."

The Lord promised to bring believing Gentiles, including eunuchs and foreigners, into a place of blessing. However, the false religious leaders will be judged, as will all the idolaters who practice immorality. But the righteous remnant, those who are humble of heart, will enjoy God's peace.

Restoration of True Worship (58:1–14)

God only legislated one fast in the Old Testament—the Day of Atonement (Lev. 23:27–32); however, during the captivity the Jews initiated several other fasts that God had not ordained (Zech. 7:3, 5; 8:19).

Exhibition of False Worship (58:1–5). Because of the hypocrisy in worship and fasting, the Lord instructed Isaiah to recite the people's sins to them aloud—with the voice of a trumpet (v. 1). Although they sought the Lord daily and went through the mechanics of worship, it was nothing more than an empty ritual (v. 2). Their motives were impure. They sought to impress God with their fasting, but despite their fasting they were busy oppressing their fellow workers (v. 3)! They also quarreled and fought with one another; yet they outwardly bowed their heads like a blade of grass and put on sackcloth and ashes (vv. 4–5). They called this a fast! God was not pleased!

God's people know about hardship. Nehemiah had to obtain permission to return to the land (Neh. 1–2); he had to rebuild the destroyed wall (Neh. 3); he faced serious, hostile opposition (Neh. 4). Nehemiah and the people who returned to Jerusalem finished rebuilding the wall in just 52 days (Neh. 6:15). God had supernaturally strengthened them (Neh. 6:16).

Definition of True Worship (58:6–7). God defined the kind of fast He wanted from His people. True fasting would result in freeing oppressed people, feeding the hungry, housing the homeless, and clothing the naked.

Blessing of True Worship (58:8–14). Those who approach the Lord in contrition and humility (57:15) will enjoy His blessing, healing, righteousness, and answered prayer (vv. 8–9). If they demonstrate their righteousness by refraining from oppressing and accusing others and instead feed the hungry and help the suffering, then God will bless them (vv. 9–10). Then the Lord will guide them safely back to the land and prosper them in the land (v. 11). He will strengthen them to rebuild their homes and cities (v. 12). If they observe the Sabbath and delight themselves in the Lord, then He will allow them to possess the land and prosper them in it (vv. 13–14).

Private and public worship can degenerate into a meaningless, mechanical exercise. What can I do to keep my worship authentic and fresh? How can I avoid hypocrisy and mere outward formality? It becomes a matter of the heart. I need to meditate thoughtfully on the Scriptures. Meditating in the Psalms is a great help. I must concentrate on the Lord in Scripture meditation and in prayer (Josh. 1:8; Ps. 1:2).

Israel was guilty of practicing fasting and religious rituals without reality. They fought and quarreled despite their fastings. If they would return to the Lord and keep the Sabbath, He would bring them into the land amid His blessings.

Confession of Israel (59:1–21)

The prophet explains why the blessings of chapter 58 have not come; it is because of Israel's sins.

Transgression of the Nation (59:1–8). The reason why Israel had not been saved and rescued from Babylon was not due to the Lord's inability to save them. He was sufficiently powerful. But because of the nation's sins, the Lord had not answered their prayers for Him to rescue them (vv. 1–2; Prov. 28:9). The Lord detailed their sins in verses 3–8. They were guilty of murder (vv. 3, 7), lying (v. 3), dishonesty, evil plotting (v. 4), violence (v. 6), injustice (v. 8). Their evil was symbolized by snakes' eggs and a spider's web—the result is death (v. 5). These verses characterize the depravity of man (cp. Rom. 3:16–17; see vv. 10–23).

Confession of the Nation (59:9–15a). The prophet identified with the nation in confessing its sinfulness. (Note the personal pronouns: "us," "we" [vv. 9–11], "our" [v. 12]. Isaiah decried the lack of justice (v. 9). For this reason the nation was not delivered from Babylon (v. 11). Isaiah confessed the sinfulness of the nation (v. 12). They were in darkness, symbolizing their spiritual estate. Justice, righteousness, and truth had left this sinful nation (v. 14).

Interposition of God (59:15b–21). The Lord saw Israel's helpless estate and there was no one to save the nation. So the Lord Himself will rescue the nation. Like a warrior going out to battle, the Lord will put on righteousness and salvation and a cloak of vengeance with a mantle of zeal—He will rescue Israel from captivity in Babylon. He will punish Israel's adversaries (v. 18) so the Gentile nations will fear Israel's God when He comes against them like a rushing river and a powerful wind (v. 19). Israel will repent, meeting the condition for the Lord to rescue them (v. 20). The final fulfillment of this rescue will be Israel's repentance and blessing at the Second Coming of Christ when the millennial kingdom is inaugurated (Rom. 11:25–26). Then the Lord will inaugurate His covenant with Israel (Jer. 31:31–34) when He pours out His Spirit on them (Ezek. 36:27; Joel 2:29).

- *The Lord was powerful enough to save Israel, but the nation's sins were the cause of Israel's suffering in captivity. When the nation repents, the Lord will rescue the nation from captivity, prefiguring Israel's ultimate rescue at the Second Coming of Jesus Christ.*

Our total depravity is not a pretty picture—not something we like to think about. Yet apart from Christ's salvation and the Holy Spirit's work within us, all of us are capable of the works of the flesh (Gal. 5:19–21). It is only as we walk in the power of the Holy Spirit that we can manifest the fruit of the Spirit (Gal. 5:22–23).

Exaltation of Jerusalem (60:1–22)

Its Light to the Nations (60:1–3). Because the Redeemer, the Messiah, comes to Jerusalem (59:20), the Shekinah glory of God will emanate from the city. The light of God's truth will spread from Jerusalem to the nations of the world in the millennium. The nations will come to Jerusalem to receive God's truth (2:2; 9:2; Zech. 14:16).

Its Wealth from the Nations (60:4–9). Israelites who were living in foreign lands would return to Israel (vv. 4, 9); Gentile nations will pay homage, bringing their wealth to Israel (vv. 4–5; 18:7; 45:14; 61:6; 66:12; Zech. 14:14–15). Camels from Midian and Ephah; gold and frankincense from Sheba; sheep from Kedar and rams from Nebaioth; produce from Tarshish—these will result in great wealth flowing into Israel.

The nations mentioned that bring their wealth to Israel are Midian, south of the Dead Sea; Ephah, descendants of the Midianites (Gen. 25:4); Sheba, southwest Arabia (modern Yemen); Kedar, northern Arabia; Nebaioth, an Arabian tribe (Gen. 25:13); and Tarshish, Spain.

Israel's Subjection of the Nations (60:10–14). Because the Lord has compassion on Israel, He will motivate foreign nations to help rebuild Jerusalem (v. 10). In the millennial kingdom,

Israel will be the preeminent nation in the world. Jerusalem will enjoy peace without fear of enemies, as the foreign nations constantly bring their tribute (v. 11). Those who attempt to rebel will be destroyed (v. 12). Lebanon will supply Israel with its choice lumber to build the millennial Temple (Ezek. 40–43), while Israel's former enemies will be subject to Israel's authority (v. 14).

Its Glory for the Nations (60:15–22). Although Israel suffered in the past, the nation will be the cause of pride in the future when the Lord will shower His blessing on it. Israel will receive the wealth of nations, like a nursing child from its mother (v. 16). Multiplied wealth from nations—gold and silver—will flow from foreign countries to Israel. Yet the nation will enjoy physical peace and spiritual righteousness (v. 17). Enemies will no longer assault the chosen people of God. The Lord God Himself will light the nation with His glory (v. 19). Israel's suffering will be over. The people will walk in righteousness, inhabit the land, and fulfill the covenant promises (Gen. 12:1–3). The Lord will bless the people spiritually and materially in the land (vv. 21–22).

In Jerusalem stands a sobering museum, Yad Vashem, depicting the horrendous torture, suffering, and death of millions of Jews during the Holocaust in World War II. The Jewish people have suffered as no other people have suffered in human history. It is imperative that we love the Jewish people and share the gospel with them (Rom. 1:16).

- *When Israel repents, the Lord will bless the nation as the Messiah returns to Israel, regathers the Jews from foreign lands, and brings them into the land to prosper them. All the nations of the world will be subject to Israel in that day and bring their wealth to Israel.*

Mission of the Messiah (61:1–11)

His First Coming: To Herald Good News (61:1–2a). Jesus read Isaiah 61:1–2a in the synagogue in Nazareth, concluding with the words, "Today this Scripture has been fulfilled in your hearing" (Luke 4:21, NASB). Jesus applied Isaiah 61:1–2a to Himself and thereby claimed to be the Messiah prophesied in that Old Testament passage. In His earthly ministry, Jesus fulfilled Isaiah's prophecy when He preached the Good News. Jesus brought redemption and release from the bondage of sin (Rom. 8:1–4). But it is noteworthy that Jesus stopped in the middle of verse 2. It becomes apparent that Isaiah's prophecy combined the first and second comings of Christ. The prophets viewed the two comings of Christ like two mountain peaks; from a distance they appeared to be the same peak, but on coming closer it became apparent there was a large valley between them. The first and second comings are separated by a large span of time, by now, about two thousand years.

All three members of the Trinity are mentioned in verse 1. "Spirit" refers to the Holy Spirit; "Lord God" refers to the Father; "me" refers to Jesus the Messiah. The Holy Spirit coming upon Christ further indicates that "me" refers to the Messiah (Matt. 3:16; 12:18; Luke 4:18; John 1:32).

His Second Coming: To Honor Israel (61:2b–11). "The day of vengeance" belongs to the Second Coming of Christ when He will judge the rebellious nations of the world (Rev. 19:15). At His Second Coming, Christ will comfort those who mourn—particularly the Jewish people who mourn over their sin (Zech. 12:10–14; Matt. 24:30). They will be comforted with a garland of joy and the oil of gladness as they enter the millennial kingdom (v. 3; Matt. 25:21, 23).

When Christ returns, Israel will be in the land in faith; Messiah will bless the nation by enabling them to rebuild the destroyed cities (vv. 4–9). Foreigners will be subject to Israel (v. 5) and

God's truth will spread from Jerusalem (v. 6a; 2:3). Israel will enjoy the wealth from other nations as they bring their tribute to Israel (v. 6b; Zech. 16:14–15). The Lord will bless Israel by fulfilling the new (everlasting) covenant in which He forgives Israel (Jer. 32:40; 31:34). In that future millennium, all the nations of the world will recognize that the Lord is blessing Israel (v. 9).

The nation of Israel bursts forth in praise as the Lord imputes His righteousness to the nation (vv. 10–11; Rom. 11:26). As a bride and groom are beautifully clothed for their sacred day, so Israel is clothed with true righteousness.

- *When Messiah returns, Israel will repent and be spiritually restored. Then Messiah will bless Israel with victory over its enemies and prosperity in the land. The nation will live in true righteousness.*

Restoration of Zion (62:1–63:6)

This section deals with Israel's restoration and blessing under Christ's rule in the millennial kingdom.

Its Glory Among the Nations (62:1–5). When Messiah returns, Israel will gain its place of preeminence among the nations—but it will be based on its righteousness. The condition upon which the Lord will bless Israel is its repentance. The tribulation will be the means by which the Lord brings Israel to repentance (Jer. 30:7); then the nation will receive the Lord's righteousness (Isa. 62:2) and be called by a new name, "married" (v. 4) and "holy" (v. 12). In that day Israel will be the crown under Messiah's rule (v. 3).

The land will no longer be desolate—destroyed by invaders, but as the wife of the Lord, Israel will enjoy the Lord's special favor (vv. 4–5; Hos. 2:16, 19).

A watchman was posted on the wall of a city to watch for an approaching enemy. He would scan the horizon for an invader and if an enemy approached, he would sound the alarm to warn the city of an impending attack. He would never sleep while on lookout.

Its Peace Within the Land (62:6–9). Spiritual watchmen, who long for Jerusalem's peace, are commanded to pray unceasingly for its peace, reminding the Lord of the promises He has made to bring peace and prosperity to Jerusalem (vv. 6–7). These praying watchmen are to continue this unceasing praying "till he establishes Jerusalem and makes her the praise of the earth" (v. 7). And God has promised to do that. He has promised a future day when Israel will no longer experience invaders who destroy the nation's crops and pillage the land. In the millennium Israel will enjoy the fruit of its labors (v. 9).

It is biblical and proper to pray for things God has commanded He will do. When Daniel saw that the seventy years of captivity that God had promised were completed, Daniel prayed that God would do what He had promised (Dan. 9:2– 3). These watchmen prayed similarly (vv. 6–9). We too, can pray that the Lord will do as He has promised on our behalf (Matt. 7:7–8; Phil. 4:6–7; 1 Pet. 5:7).

Its Salvation from the Lord (62:10–12). The return of the Lord is anticipated. Israel is called to prepare spiritually for the Lord's return (cp. 40:3–4). A flag will be raised for all the nations to see, declaring Messiah's return (v. 10). And when He comes, He will bless Israel, the spiritually renewed people. They will be a holy people, redeemed by Christ (v. 12), fulfilling their original purpose (Exod. 19:6).

Its Subjugation of the Enemies (63:1–6). The Lord is pictured coming as a victorious, conquering general. He comes from having judged Edom and Bozrah, a city of Edom, because the Edomites were enemies who had afflicted Israel (Obad. 1–21; Mal. 1:4). The Lord's garments are red, splattered with the blood of the enemies He has conquered (vv. 2–3). When He returns, Messiah will avenge Israel (v. 4; Joel 3:1–3). The battle of Armageddon is described (v. 6; Zech. 14:1–4; Rev. 16:14, 16; Rev. 19:11–21).

During the grape harvest, the Israelites would place the grapes in a large vat. Amid celebration and singing, they would crush the grapes with their bare feet. The juice would run into a lower vat. Crushing grapes was a symbol the Lord used to depict His crushing of the enemy (Rev. 14:19–20; 19:15).

The Jewish people stand in a special place of blessing (Rom. 11). They are forever God's special people; God has never abrogated His promises to them (Rom. 11:29). We should pray for the peace of Jerusalem and reach out to the Jewish people.

- *Messiah will return, conquer Israel's enemies,*
- *and restore Israel to a place of preeminence*
- *above the nations of the world. Israel will*
- *enjoy safety and peace; foreign nations will no*
- *longer invade the land. The Lord will conquer*
- *and subdue all the nations of the world.*

Petition of Israel (63:7–64:12)

The righteous remnant, in captivity in Babylon, prayed to the Lord in a seemingly hopeless situation.

Consideration of the Past (63:7–14). Isaiah prayed on behalf of the nation (representing the remnant), looking to the past when the Lord exhibited His lovingkindness and delivered the nation from Egyptian bondage. He became their Savior, their deliverer from oppression when the angel of the Lord rescued them (vv. 8–9; Exod. 23:20–23). But Israel rebelled against the Lord (Exod. 17:1–7), so He chastened them (v. 10). Then they remembered how the Lord used Moses to deliver them from Egypt, bringing them safely through the Red Sea by miraculously dividing the waters (vv. 11–12; Exod. 14:21–31). The Lord brought them safely into the land and gave them rest (v. 14; Josh. 21:43–45).

Lovingkindness

The word translated "lovingkindness" is the Hebrew word *hesed*, which means "loyal love." It expresses God's faithfulness to His covenant people, Israel. Despite Israel's unfaithfulness (Hos. 4:1; 6:4, 6), the Lord was faithful in His covenant relationship with them (Isa. 63:7).

Petition Concerning the Present (63:15–64:12). The remnant pleaded for the Lord to deliver them from captivity, asking Him once again to display His power on their behalf (v. 15). They prayed on the basis of their relationship: God was their Father (v. 16; cp. Matt. 6:9). They begged the Lord to restore them spiritually; they were His special people who once worshiped in the Temple in Jerusalem, the Temple that the Babylonians destroyed (v. 18).

The remnant pleaded for God's power to be demonstrated in judgment (64:1–3). They petitioned God to tear the heavens like a curtain, to come down and demonstrate His power and His presence just as He did on Mt. Sinai (v. 3; Exod. 19:16–20). Then the nations would tremble in fear (v. 2).

God is unequalled; He has no peer, yet He seeks fellowship with those who trust Him (v. 4). But sin presents a problem. All the righteous formalities are like filthy rags, and sin carries them away like the wind drives the dried leaves (v. 6). And yet no one bothers to come to the Lord for mercy (v. 7)!

People generally do not fear God today. Why not? Why don't they stand in awe of His greatness? Probably the problem relates to our concept of ourselves. We are more intent with developing a "healthy self-image" than having a biblical view of ourselves. Verse 6 is not a pretty verse—but it is biblical! Perhaps if we recognized who we really are apart from God's intervening grace, we would have a greater fear of and reverence for God.

On the basis of their relationship—God is their Father—the remnant pleaded for the Lord to restore them (vv. 8–12). They cried out because Jerusalem was desolate like the desert; Solomon's glorious temple had been destroyed by fire (v. 11; 2 Kings 25:9). Would the Lord continue to punish them in Babylon? Would He hold Himself back or would He rescue them (v. 12)?

Explanation of God (65:1–25)

This chapter records the Lord's response to the remnant's prayer.

Indictment of Israel (65:1–7). In answer to the remnant's prayer, the Lord reminded them that He had constantly been extending His hands in mercy to the nation but they didn't bother to call on Him; they were rebellious (v. 2; cp. Rom. 10:20–21). They indulged in idolatry, provoking the Lord when they committed sexual immorality in the gardens (v. 3; cp. 1:29; 57:5;

66:17). They practiced necromancy as they consulted with the dead sitting among the graves (v. 4; cp. 8:19). They scorned the Mosaic Law by eating pork and other unclean meats (v. 4; cp. Lev. 11:7). Yet these people claimed they were righteous. It was a stench in God's nostrils (v. 5)! He would indeed repay them! They would pay for their own sins and the sins of their fathers because they were all alike: guilty of idolatry (v. 7; cp. 57:7). They would be judged.

Six to twelve miles in width, Sharon is the fertile coastal plain extending from Joppa to Mt. Carmel in the north. It was known for its floral beauty (Song 2:1; Isa. 35:20) as well as grazing land for cattle (1 Chron. 27:29). The valley of Achor, ten miles south of Jericho, became proverbial for hope and blessing.

Election of Israel (65:8–16). But God promised not to destroy them. Instead, He would preserve a remnant, like good grapes plucked from among the bad (v. 8). The godly remnant would inherit the land and enjoy the Lord's peace and prosperity in the land (vv. 9–10). But the apostates will be punished (vv. 11–12). They wanted to know the future by presenting offerings to Fortune, the Syrian god of good luck and destiny, the pagan god of fate—they would themselves be destined (a play on words) for death (v. 12).

The Lord will ultimately separate the righteous remnant from the rebellious people (vv. 13–16). His servants will eat, drink, and rejoice in the land; they will be given another name because they are children of the God of truth (v. 16; cp. John 14:6). The rebels will not enjoy the fruit of the land. Isaiah is probably looking forward to the future when the righteous remnant will inherit the millennial kingdom and enjoy Messiah's blessing (cp. Matt. 25:10, 21, 23), but the unrighteous will be cast out (Matt. 25:12, 30).

Blessing of Israel (65:17–25). Isaiah looked into the future, that glorious day when Israel will be restored to the land under Messiah's rule, enjoying peace and prosperity in the millennial kingdom. Whereas Rev. 21:4 indicates the new heavens and the new earth follow the millennial kingdom and describe the eternal state, Isaiah likely merges the concepts of the millennial kingdom and the eternal state. In any case, these are conditions that will be prevalent during the millennial kingdom.

Joy will be prevalent in Messiah's kingdom (vv. 17–19). Since there will be no sickness or suffering, weeping and crying will vanish (v. 19). There will be longevity in the kingdom (v. 20; Zech. 8:4–5). Those who become believers during the tribulation will enter the millennial kingdom in their earthly bodies; they will procreate and those born in the millennium will need to trust in Christ for salvation. Those who do not believe and who attempt to rebel will be judged in death (v. 20).

It appears that believers will not die during the millennium. The land will be productive during the millennium; there will be bumper crops (vv. 21–22; Amos 9:13). No enemy will pillage their crops (v. 22). Israel will live in security and peace in the millennium (vv. 23–25). Children will not suffer. If there is a need, they will call on the Lord and He will respond (v. 24). The animal kingdom will be at peace (11:6–9). From Jerusalem extending throughout the world, the Messiah will rule; peace will prevail.

Blessing in the Kingdom (66:1–24)

This chapter brings the book of Isaiah to a close, describing the millennium and true worship under Messiah's rule. It emphasizes God's greatness and the need for people to repent to enjoy fellowship with Him.

Condemnation of False Worship (66:1–6). The Lord is pictured as enthroned, ruling as king in the millennium. Although He is so majestic that no earthly temple could contain Him, yet He condescends to fellowship with those who are humble and heed His word (v. 2). But the Lord, who sees the heart, condemns hypocritical worship (vv. 3–6; 1:11–15). Despite their offerings (v. 3), the hypocrites ignored the Lord and sinned against Him (v. 4), hence, the Lord would punish them for their sin (v. 4). But the remnant feared the Lord and trembled at His word—and they were hated because of it (v. 5). For that the Lord would judge them by allowing the Babylonians to destroy the Temple (v. 6).

Consolation of True Worshipers (66:7–24). The remnant is comforted; Jerusalem will be restored! As quickly as a woman giving birth even before labor pains, so Jerusalem will be restored (vv. 7–8). God does not begin something without finishing it (v. 9)! As certain as a woman opening her womb for delivery, so God will restore Jerusalem.

Looking beyond the historic restoration of Jerusalem in 538 B.C., the prophet looked to the future when Jerusalem would enjoy permanent peace (vv. 10–14). It is a cause of rejoicing. Like a mother nourishing her infant, so Jerusalem will be prosperous, nourishing its people (v. 11). Jerusalem will be preeminent, exalted above the nations as the supreme city of the world (v. 12; 2:2). The wealth of other nations will flow to Jerusalem (v. 13; 60:5; 61:6; Zech. 14:14–15), and its inhabitants will rejoice (vv. 13–14).

When the Lord comes to bless Jerusalem He will also judge the rebels, those who were guilty of idolatry and repudiation of His word (vv. 15–18; Matt. 25:32; 2 Thess. 1:7–9; Rev. 19:15–19). The Lord's judgment will extend to the nations (v. 18; Matt. 25:32).

In that climactic day, the Lord will rescue the believing remnant, who will spread the news of God's glory to the distant nations (v. 19). They will be the Lord's final missionaries, carrying the knowledge of Him to Europe, Asia, and Africa. But the Jews who were scattered among the nations will return to Jerusalem to worship God on His "holy mountain," Jerusalem. In that day all nations will acknowledge the Lord and bow before His great name (v. 22; Phil. 2:10). But those who repudiate the Lord will be cast into everlasting torment (v. 24; Dan. 12:2; Matt. 8:12; 24:51; 25:30, 46). Isaiah ends the book on a somber note, emphasizing the need for repentance and a genuine response of the heart to the Lord's gracious invitation.

The nations of verse 19 may be identified as follows: Tarshish likely represents Spain; Put is Libya; Lud is Lydia in Asia Minor; Tubal is usually identified with Meshech (Ezek. 38:2–3); Rosh is southeast of the Black Sea; Javan is Greece.

■ *The Lord promised to restore the Jews from*
■ *captivity in Babylon and He will certainly do*
■ *so. This restoration prefigures the ultimate*
■ *blessing of Jerusalem in the millennial kingdom*
■ *when the Lord returns to rescue and bless the*
■ *believing remnant and judge the rebels.*

QUESTIONS TO GUIDE YOUR STUDY

1. What picture did Isaiah use (49:14–26) to describe how precious Israel is to God?
2. What were some of the reasons the Servant was not recognized by some and rejected by others?
3. Who did God hold responsible for Israel's moral failure?
4. On what occasion did Jesus quote Isaiah 61:1–2a?
5. What does the restoration of Israel from Babylon prefigure?

Perhaps the overwhelming lesson of Isaiah is the sinfulness of man and the mercy of God. The lesson of Isaiah is also the lesson of the Bible—man continues in rebellion against God and God continues to extend mercy and grace. What can we learn from this? God desires a humble and contrite heart (66:2). Nothing pleases Him more. And those are the ones who will enjoy intimate fellowship with Him.

SHEPHERD'S
NOTES